GCSE
Computer Science (AQA)

2nd edition

Susan Robson

Published by

PG Online Limited

The Old Coach House

35 Main Road

Tolpuddle

Dorset DT2 7EW

Email sales@pgonline.co.uk

Website www.pgonline.co.uk

GCSE Computer Science (AQA)

Design and artwork by Direction   www.direction123.com

Cover image © 'Free Air' by Neil Canning

www.neilcanning.com

First edition 2012

Second Edition 2014

A catalogue entry for this book is available from the British Library

ISBN 978-1-910523-01-8

Printed and Bound in Great Britain by Lightning Source, Milton Keynes

Preface

The aim of this book is to provide comprehensive yet concise coverage of all the topics covered in Component 2 of *AQA Computer Science 4512*, on which the written examination is based. It is written in clear and easily understandable English and will be invaluable not only as a course textbook but also as a revision guide.

It is divided into seven chapters covering every element of the specification, each ending with a "Glossary of Terms" and exam-style questions similar to those which are likely to appear on final exam papers. Answers to all questions, with hints and tips on how to tackle them, are given at the end of the book.

The book is also available as a downloadable PDF, sold as a lifetime site licence to schools. This PDF may be loaded onto the school's private network or VLE.

To accompany this textbook, PG Online also publishes a series of seven downloadable teaching units. Each lesson in a unit consists of a PowerPoint presentation, teacher's notes, worksheets to be completed during the lesson and homework sheets with exam-style questions. These units are sold as a lifetime site licence and may be loaded onto the school's private network or VLE.

For more information on the PDF version of the book and the teaching units, please visit **www.pgonline.co.uk**

About the author

Susan Robson has a degree in Computer Science from Manchester University and a PGCE from Portsmouth University. She worked for International Computers Ltd (pre Fujitsu days) straight out of university, followed by 12 years in technical pre-sales and then sales for ECI Telecom before moving into teaching Computing at Queen Mary's Sixth Form College, Basingstoke. She is currently Head of Computing at Bedales in Petersfield where she teaches GCSE and A Level Computing courses.

PG ONLINE

Table of Contents

Table of Contents

Chapter 1: Fundamentals of Computer Systems

This chapter describes the basic components of a computer system, the impact of using computers in the modern world and issues that arise from this.

Computer Systems

The AQA specification says that students should:

- be able to define a computer system (i.e. hardware and software working together to create a working solution)

- be able to describe and explain the fundamental pieces of hardware required to make a functioning computer system

A computer system is made up of hardware and software. Hardware is any physical component that makes up the computer. Software is any program that runs on the computer. Together these create a working solution to a problem.

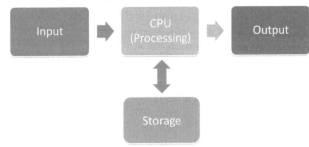

Computer systems are all around us. They are not just the PCs on the desk but include mobile phones, cash machines, supermarket tills and the engine management systems in a modern-day car. The diagram to the right shows the basic model of any computer system.

All computer systems must have at least one **input device** that gets data from the real-world. This could be a mouse and keyboard on a conventional PC but could be a temperature sensor (thermistor) in a commercial greenhouse or the microphone on a mobile phone. Input devices take real-world data and convert it into a form that can be stored on the computer.

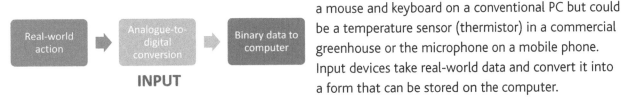

The input from these devices is processed and the computer system will generate outputs. The **output device** could be, for example, a conventional computer screen, an actuator that opens or closes a greenhouse window or the speaker that produces sound on a phone.

The fourth component is **storage**. The computer system may need to use stored data to perform the processing and, as a result of processing input, may generate data that is then stored.

Any computer system will have these four basic components. They will be discussed in more detail in *Chapter 2: Hardware*.

Importance of Computers

The AQA specification says that students should:

- understand and be able to discuss the importance of computer systems to the modern world

- understand that computer systems must be reliable and robust and be able to discuss the reasons why this is important

Think about all of the places you go in the course of a day and all the computer systems you see. Computers are embedded in household appliances such as fridges and microwave ovens. Your mobile phone, TV and games console are also computer systems. When you ride in a car, a computer system is controlling the engine as well as the car's GPS, windows and stereo.

We are becoming increasingly dependent on computer systems at school, at work and at home. Consider what problems you would have if all of these computers stopped working. If the games console didn't work you might be upset but it wouldn't be a big problem. If the network at school went down you wouldn't be able to get to any of the resources and teachers wouldn't be able to show you their slides or use smart-whiteboards. If there are problems with computer systems in shops they can't sell anything and if bank systems have problems, people cannot access their money, or worse still, other people can!

? For you to find out...

Look at some websites to find stories about computer systems failures.

If computer-controlled signage on motorways goes wrong there could be health and safety implications. If computer systems in hospitals go wrong people could die. The reliability of computer systems is extremely important. In some situations reliability is more important than how quickly they work or how many features they have.

Measuring Reliability

How do you know how reliable a computer system is? We talk about system **availability** meaning the percentage of time it is available for. For example, if a system is down (unavailable) for 1 hour in a 100 hour period, then the system availability is 99% for this period. Normally equipment manufacturers will quote average availability over a long period of time.

Another way of measuring a system's reliability is to measure the length of time between system failures. **MTBF** is the **Mean Time Between Failure** and is quoted by equipment manufacturers as an indication of reliability.

Robustness – protecting against system failures

Another aspect of reliability is how robust the equipment is. In terms of computer systems, robustness is about how tolerant the system is to failure. In a "robust" system, a single failure will not take the whole system down. A robust system may also be described as **fault-tolerant**.

Hardware redundancy is one way to protect systems. This means having more than one of each critical component. For example, computer systems in commercial aircraft have triple redundancy; three separate identical computer systems control each major function so that if one or even two systems fail, the third will hopefully get you to your destination safely.

In general, if software or hardware problems occur, it is the data which is most at risk. This will be stored on a disk on a server somewhere. As well as redundant hardware, companies must make sure that data is backed up regularly.

Sometimes computer systems are so important to a company that it cannot function without them. A computer system failure could mean that a company goes out of business in just a few days. **Disaster recovery** plans need to be put in place so that a company can switch over to a complete new system with all its own data on it, often within hours. There are disaster recovery companies that specialise in offering this service to companies who depend on their computer systems.

> **? For you to find out...**
>
> Look up "RAID computer storage" to see how companies protect their computer systems against disk failure.

Issues Relating to the Use of Computer Technology

The AQA specification says that students should:

- evaluate the impact of and issues related to the use of computer technology in society

There are several legal, ethical and environmental issues related to the use of computer technology in society.

Legal issues

All computer systems must meet legal requirements. Listed below are some of the laws relating to computer systems.

- **The Data Protection Act** says that anyone who stores personal details must keep them secure. Companies with computer systems that store any personal data must have processes and security mechanisms designed into the system to meet this requirement.

  Many people worry about the data that is stored about them and how secure it is. This is a big issue for many but the DPA is designed to protect individuals' data.

- **The Health and Safety at Work Act** makes employers responsible for their staff. Design considerations should provide appropriate working conditions for staff. Designers should consider how easy systems will be to use and any health implications there might be based on their choices of software, screen layout, input methods and the hardware used.

  Individuals using computers at work have the right to expect decent working conditions. They should have appropriate desks and chairs that are adjustable, as well as good lighting and ventilation in the office.

- **The Copyright, Designs and Patents Act** makes it illegal to use software without buying the appropriate licence. Computers have also made it very easy to download music and films illegally, and to copy say, essays or projects written by other people and available on the Internet. Universities and Exam Boards use specially written software to search for instances of plagiarism (copying other people's work).

  As an individual you should make sure that you only run licensed software on your PC at home. Technically it is theft if you just get a copy from a friend. The Copyright, Designs and Patents Act protects the people who write the software from people making illegal copies. This law is difficult to enforce and many people don't see it as stealing, even though it is illegal and you could be prosecuted.

Ethical issues

Ethical considerations are all about fairness. Here are some examples of ethical issues around computer systems:

- Is it fair that some people cannot afford computers?
- Are countries like India being exploited as a source of cheap labour for call centres and for programming?
- Should companies use local programmers and call centres?
- Does the system design disadvantage some part of the community?
- Does the system design promote accessibility for all?

Environmental issues

Environmental issues include the carbon footprint and waste products that result from manufacturing computer systems, but this is often outweighed by the positive effects on the environment of using computerised systems to manage processes that might otherwise generate more pollution.

Considerations may include:

- Does a computer system mean that people can work from home and therefore drive less?
- Does a computer system mean more manufacturing?
- Is working at home more environmentally friendly than everyone working in a big office, in terms of heating and lighting?
- Do computer-managed engines work more efficiently? Create less pollution and use less fuel?

Impact of computer technology on society

Computer technology impacts just about everything we do. Here are just a few areas to consider:

- **Communication:** Before we had computers we would phone or write letters to people. These days we use email and texting. Anywhere in the world we can use mobile technologies to send pictures and files to people almost instantly.

- **Employment:** The computer industry itself offers employment for millions of people but you should also consider how computer technology impacts jobs generally. When computer technology first started being used in the workplace, many people thought that there would be fewer jobs, because the computers would make everything much quicker and easier. In actual fact, this never really happened. The computers just meant that people had more time to do different jobs. Computers in the workplace are used for storing data, processing data and automating processes that used to take a long time. For example, a company payroll would have been done manually but would now be done on a spreadsheet or specialised payroll software in a fraction of the time. Money is transferred to employees' accounts automatically.

- **Social interaction:** Many people of all ages use social networking sites and Twitter to keep in touch with friends and family. If you are out and about, you are more likely to post a photograph and a comment on Facebook than send a postcard. You can communicate with friends and family all over world very easily. As well as keeping in touch, people use internet dating sites to meet people rather than going to bars and clubs. People game online with friends from their own houses rather than all getting together for a game of cards. Social networking using computer technology has become normal. Some people think this is great because you can have more "friends" but some people think we are losing the ability to socially interact face-to-face.

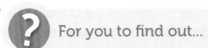
For you to find out...

In your class, find out how much time you all spend on social networking sites. Discuss if you think this is a good thing or not.

- **Shopping:** Computer technology has helped people who find it difficult to get to the shops. Supermarkets provide online shopping and deliver to the home, and you can buy just about everything on the internet these days. How has this affected the shops? CD and DVD sales have dropped in shops because more and more people buy online or just download the tracks they want. To shop online you need a credit card but it is easier to use someone else's credit card online than in a shop. This has led to an increase in credit card fraud and identity theft.

- **Manufacturing:** Computer technology is used in manufacturing to produce items cheaper and quicker than can be done by hand. A computer-regulated production line will be able to make things more consistently and within a smaller tolerance. For example, rolling out a steel plate to 2mm can be done very precisely with computer sensors giving constant feedback to the rollers. A negative effect of this may be that there is less of a market for handmade, crafted items.

- **Safety:** Many dangerous jobs can now be done by remote-controlled devices and sensors; for example, bomb disposal robots and devices which can sense poisonous gases in mines. Weather data can be collected from the top of a mountain or from inside a volcano without a scientist having to go into these dangerous situations every day to collect it.

In the exam you will need to be able to consider the positive and negative effects of using computer technology. Computers generally make processes faster, cheaper and more accurate but we also need to consider the human cost in terms of jobs, social interaction and losing the skills to make things ourselves.

Glossary of Terms

Basic Model

Computer System	A combination of hardware and software components that allow input, processing and output of data.
Hardware	The physical components that make up a computer system.
Software	The programs that run on a computer system.
Input Devices	Hardware that takes real-world analogue data and converts it into a digital form which can be stored on a computer. For example: keyboard, mouse, microphone, webcam, scanner, sensors.
Output Device	Hardware that presents the result of processing to the user or actuators that perform a task automatically. They use digital data from a computer and produce it in a form that is understandable or usable. For example: monitors, printers, speakers, actuators (motors).
Storage Device	Hardware that is used to store files long-term and is non-volatile, such as hard disks, memory sticks, magnetic tapes and CDs.

Importance of Computers

Reliability	How much you can depend on the computer system being available when you need it. Usually measured in terms of availability.
Availability	The proportion of time that a system is operational, usually expressed as a percentage over a certain period of time. For example, 95% measured over 1 year.
MTBF	Mean Time Between Failure: a measure of availability often quoted by hardware manufacturers. For example 2.56 years between failures means that, on average, the hardware can be expected to last 2.56 years before it goes wrong.
Robust	Describes a system that is resilient to failure.
Fault-Tolerant	Computer systems where redundant components stop a single failure bringing the system down.
Redundancy	Spare hardware components are built into a system so, in the event of a component failing, the system can swap over to the spare one.

Sample Questions

These questions are similar to the ones you may see in the exam. Good answers to these, along with exam hints and tips, can be found at the end of the book.

1 For each hardware device listed in the table below, place one tick in each row to show whether it is an input device or output device.   [5]

	Input	Output
Microphone		
LED (light emitting diode)		
Barcode scanner		
Speaker		
Actuator		

2 Twitter is an online social networking service that enables users to send and read short messages called "tweets". Services such as Twitter, used on mobile phones, have been used to coordinate demonstrations and riots.

Discuss **three** technical reasons why applications like Twitter may have been used for this purpose.

In this question you will be marked on your ability to use good English, to organise information clearly and to use specialist vocabulary where appropriate.   [6]

3 Fred says that computers will save the environment but Priti thinks that manufacturing the computers is damaging the environment. Explain why both could be right.

In this question you will be marked on your ability to use good English, to organise information clearly and to use specialist vocabulary where appropriate.   [6]

4 Describe **two** ways in which people commonly break the Copyright, Design and Patents Act.   [4]

Chapter 2: Hardware

In Chapter 1 we looked at the basic components of a computer system. This chapter describes the various hardware components that make up a computer system, and the developments in hardware technologies that are leading to innovative new products being developed.

The Central Processing Unit (CPU)

The AQA specification says that students should:

- be able to describe the purpose of the processor (CPU)

The **central processing unit (CPU)** of a computer is the hardware that executes programs and manages the rest of the hardware. Think of the CPU as the brain of the computer. Just as your brain contains parts that remember things, parts that think and parts that make the rest of your body operate, the CPU does the same for the computer. The CPU is made up of the main memory, the processor and the cache memory (we'll talk about the cache later). The program instructions and data move between the main memory and the processor using internal connections called **system buses**.

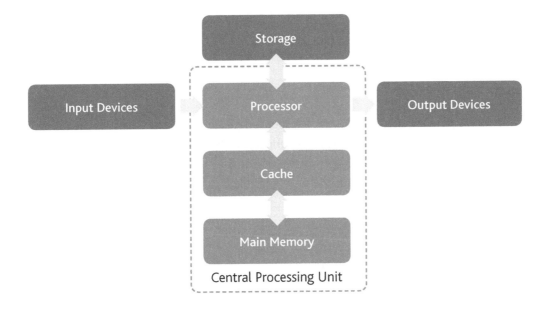

When a program is to be run (executed) on a computer it first has to be loaded into the main memory. From here it can be accessed by the processor, which executes each instruction in turn. When the program is loaded, the processor is given the start address of where the program is held in main memory. To run the program the processor fetches an instruction, decodes it and then executes it. The processor executes one instruction at a time. This is called the **fetch-execute cycle**.

Fetch an instruction from Main Memory

Decode the instruction

Execute the instruction

The purpose of the CPU can be summarised as follows:

- fetch instructions from main memory

- fetch data from main memory

- decode the instructions

- execute the instructions

- perform calculations

- manage the movement of instructions and data to and from peripheral devices

CPU Performance

The AQA specification says that students should:

- be able to explain the effect of common CPU characteristics on the performance of the processor. These should include clock speed, number of cores and cache size/types.

Clock speed

The speed at which a processor operates is the clock speed, measured in Hertz. Hertz is the name for the number of electrical cycles per second, or the rate at which the electrical current changes in the actual circuits. Everything the processor does happens on the tick of the clock, so a faster clock means that more instructions are fetched, decoded and executed in a second.

? For you to find out...

Look at some PC adverts in magazines and on the internet to get a feel for current computer specifications

The speed of the processor is quoted in MHz (Megahertz) or GHz (Gigahertz). At the time of writing (August 2014) processors in a typical home PC might be rated at 3 to 4GHz (for example, Intel's i7 is now common in home PCs and laptops).

In theory a computer with a 400 MHz processor should operate twice as fast as one with a 200MHz processor but it isn't that simple. There are lots of other components that contribute to the overall speed of the computer. Each one can create a bottleneck in the system and slow it down. Imagine a 3-lane motorway where the traffic can go really fast until it gets to a 1-lane road going into a town. No matter how many lanes you add to the motorway, the 1-lane part of the journey will limit how quickly traffic can get into town. In the same way, a slow component can slow the whole computer down.

One bottleneck that can occur is the access speed of main memory. Reading from and writing to main memory is much slower than the speed at which the processor can work. The logical answer is to use faster memory technologies but this increases the price of the computer. Modern computers run lots of programs at the same time so they need lots of memory. There needs to be a compromise between speed and cost.

Cache

One way of improving speed at minimal cost is to use a small amount of much faster memory where frequently used instructions or data can be stored for a while. We call this special sort of high-speed memory the **cache** (pronounced "cash"). If the processor has to access main memory less often it can work faster so the CPU performance increases.

A typical PC (in Aug 2014) might have 16 GB of RAM (main memory) but only 4 MB of the faster more expensive cache memory. Notice the different units here and remember that there are 1024 Megabytes in a Gigabyte. This computer therefore has 4096 times more RAM than cache memory.

There are different levels of cache memory, categorized in levels that describe its closeness and accessibility to the microprocessor:

- **Level 1 cache** (also called primary cache or internal cache)
  L1 cache is built onto the processor chip and is the fastest and most expensive cache in the computer. The L1 cache stores copies of the data and instructions from the most recently or frequently used main memory locations.

- **Level 2 cache** (also called secondary cache or external cache)
  L2 cache is commonly located on the motherboard, although with most new processors it is found on the processor chip itself.

- **Level 3 cache**
  When L2 cache is found on the processor, the cache found on the motherboard is called L3 cache.

Multi-core processors

When we looked at the basic fetch-execute cycle we assumed that there was a single processor and a single main memory. You have probably heard terms like "dual-core" and "quad-core" so where do these fit in? Today's more complex CPUs can include more than one processor, or core. A dual-core processor has two processing components within the CPU. A quad core, likewise, has four. In theory having two processors means that the computer can operate twice as fast but this isn't always the case.

Imagine a bakery where one chef is making cakes. If you brought in three more chefs they could all make their own cakes and the bakery would make four times as many cakes. If there was only one recipe, though, you couldn't have Cook 1 doing the first line of the recipe, Cook 2 doing line 2, Cook 3 doing line 3 and so on. Cook 2 would need to wait for the first cook to mix the flour and butter before he could fold in the eggs! So four cooks working their way through one recipe wouldn't be any quicker, in fact it would be more complicated (you've heard the saying "Too many cooks spoil the broth"). Likewise a program is a series of instructions that need to be done in order. Multiple processors could work on different programs that operate in parallel but unless the computer is designed to use multiple cores it isn't necessarily four times faster. On the whole, though, a PC with lots of programs going on at the same time will have a multiple-core processor and will operate faster than a single-core processor.

Connecting CPU Components with System Buses

The AQA specification says that students should:

- understand how different components link to a processor (ROM, RAM, I/O, storage, etc)

The components in the CPU are connected together using three **system buses**. A bus is a bit like a cable; it consists of lots of separate parallel wires going from one component to another. On the motherboard of a computer these wires are built into the printed circuit board. The picture to the right shows a chip with all its metal pins connecting it into the motherboard. Notice the lines etched in the board that lead to each pin. These lines are fine wires embedded in the board and groups of these form a **bus**.

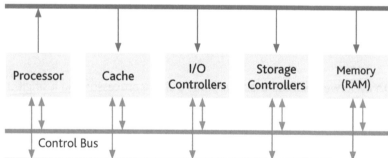

Address Bus

Processor | Cache | I/O Controllers | Storage Controllers | Memory (RAM)

Control Bus

Data Bus

When a program is running, the processor will get one instruction at a time from main memory. The "fetch" part of the fetch-execute cycle consists of the processor sending the address of the next instruction to main memory using a one-way **address bus**. The instruction at that location in memory is then sent to the processor over the **data bus**.

The data bus is two-way as the processor may need to send data back to main memory or to secondary storage. The data bus and address bus connect several components together within the CPU but only one component can transmit at any one time. The control bus carries signals that show if the data bus and address bus are already in use.

Memory

Memory in a computer system refers to the components that store (or remember) instructions and data. There are different types of memory with different purposes. Some are very fast and expensive such as the cache memory discussed earlier, and some are cheaper and slower such as the memory sticks you probably use at school.

These different types of memory have different characteristics and can be compared in terms of their access speed (how quickly you can read from them or write to them), their price and the whether they can store data when the power is turned off (volatility). Let's consider some common types of memory in computer systems:

Random Access Memory (RAM)

RAM is the type of memory used in the computer's main memory. Many people say "RAM" when they mean main memory. Nothing in a computer is really "random" so random access just refers to the fact that you can write anywhere in that memory space at any time, you don't have to put the next thing straight after the last one like you do on a magnetic tape, for example.

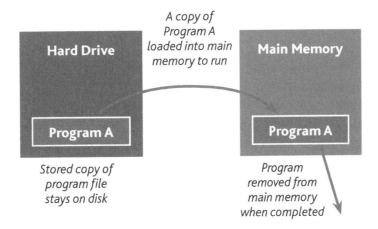

As we said earlier in the chapter, when a program is running it has to be loaded from the hard disk into main memory so that the processor can access the instructions. Any data needed for that program to run is also loaded into main memory while the program is running. The main purpose of RAM is to act as temporary storage for programs and data, just for the duration of that program. Once the program has finished and is closed, it is no longer held in main memory.

Virtual Memory

Sometimes there just isn't enough main memory for all the programs that need to run. Computers can be configured so that part of the hard disk behaves like main memory. This is called **virtual memory**. The access speed on a hard disk is much slower than the speed of RAM so this isn't ideal. It is used to store parts of programs currently being run, but the parts actually being executed still need to be in main memory. As the processor gets to the next part of the program, sections

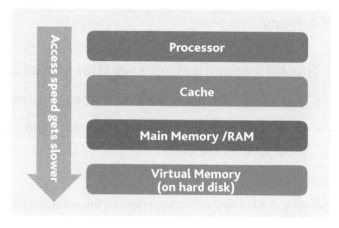

are swapped between virtual memory and main memory. Sometimes this works well but sometimes the computer spends more time swapping bits around than it does executing the program!

Read-Only Memory (ROM)

RAM is volatile so when you turn off your computer it loses its contents. When you turn the computer back on it needs to get the basic startup routine from somewhere that is not volatile. The operating system and all your programs will be stored on the hard disk but these need to be loaded into RAM to run.

The computer has a piece of software called the **bootstrap loader**. This is a small program that loads the operating system. Once the operating system is loaded it takes care of the rest. The term comes from the idea that when you're not doing very well in life you can "pull yourself up by your bootstraps". In this day and age you're more likely to hear "sort yourself out" but the meaning is the same – you are in effect getting yourself restarted. Bootstrapping became abbreviated to booting, a term you have probably heard before. To "boot" a computer is to start it up from scratch.

ROM is **Read-Only Memory**; you cannot write over the contents once it has been created. It is also non-volatile; you can leave the computer switched off for months and it will still s n the other hand is only used for temporary storage of programs when they are running. RAM is read-write and volatile.

ROM	RAM
Read only	Read – write
Not volatile	Volatile

Secondary Memory

Main memory is also known as **Primary Memory** or **Immediate Access Store**. Memory is all about storage so, strictly speaking, storage devices such as hard disks and memory sticks (also called USB flash drives) are also a type of memory. These long term, non volatile types of storage are also called **Secondary Memory**.

Typically a PC will have a hard disk that stores all the files long term. Secondary memory/storage also includes memory sticks, floppy disks (seldom used these days), tapes, CDs and DVDs. These are discussed further in the next section.

Volatility

The AQA specification says that students should:

• know the differences between non-volatile and volatile memory

When you are in the middle of a piece of work at school and your "friend" turns the computer off you will notice that you lose the work you did since you last saved. This is because the saved version goes onto the hard disk but the most recent version was only in main memory/RAM when the power went off. RAM is described as **volatile**; it loses its contents if there is no power. The hard disk is designed for long term storage of files and is **non-volatile** memory.

Secondary Storage

The AQA Specification says that you should be able to:

• understand what secondary storage is and be able to explain why it is required

• be able to describe the most common types of secondary storage

• understand how optical media, magnetic media and solid state work

We all want to store files over a long period of time. We keep photographs, projects, music, films, letters and spreadsheets on our computers. We also expect our programs to be there when we switch the computer on. This long term storage is sometimes called Secondary Memory or Secondary Storage (primary memory is the main memory). Typically a PC will have a hard disk that stores all the files long term but secondary memory/ storage also includes memory sticks, tapes and CDs.

Secondary storage is usually much larger and, as we want such a lot of it, needs to be cheap. Cheaper memory technologies tend to have slower access speeds than main memory, as discussed earlier. Secondary memory is non-volatile and needs to be robust and reliable. Has your memory stick been through the washing machine yet?

Choosing the right type of storage medium for a particular use is important. You need to consider the following features:

Capacity: How much space there is to store files.

Speed: How quickly the computer can read data from a storage device or write data to it.

Portability: Can you easily unplug it and carry it away? Does it fit in a pencil case/handbag?

Durability: How easily is it damaged? Will it survive dropping or having coffee tipped on it?

Reliability: How long will it last? Anything with moving parts is likely to be less reliable.

Magnetic storage media

This is the oldest of the technologies and is used in hard disks and tapes.

It is cheap and high capacity (stores a lot of data). Magnetic disks are read with a moving head inside the disk drive and magnetic tapes are read by moving the tape past a read-write head. Moving parts make these media quite slow to read from or write to and moving parts go wrong more often than solid state media. Magnetic media are also vulnerable to damage as well. Just as a video tape left on a stereo speaker is damaged by the magnets, so too a magnetic disk or tape can be easily wiped.

	MAGNETIC STORAGE DEVICES		
	Internal Hard Disk	Portable Hard Disk	Magnetic Tape
Cost	Very cheap but not as cheap as tape 3TB internal for £95		Cheapest bulk data storage medium 1.5TB tape £23
Capacity	Up to 4TB		
Access Speed	3Gb/s	480Mb/s (speed of USB2 interface)	Slow access speed because tape drive has to read through the tape serially
Portability	Not portable, built into PC	Can fit in a large pocket	Cassette tape is compact but needs a tape drive to use
Durability	Good durability when disk not in use but vulnerable to movement when spinning. Can write to the disk an infinite number of times. Affected by heat and magnetic fields		Limited lifetime, wears out with repeated use. If used once for archiving can last 15 years. Affected by heat and magnetic fields.
Reliability	Extremely reliable		Very reliable if not damaged
Typical use	Inside a PC as secondary storage	Supplementary storage for a PC or portable storage where high capacity is required	Good for backups and archiving but access speed is too slow for general use

How magnetic media work

Whether the storage device is a tape or a disk the principle is the same and involves three key components:

The tape or disk is covered in or contains a magnetic substance (Iron Oxide or Chromium Oxide).

- On a disk the magnetic material is in circular tracks on the surface of the disk **platters** (the hard disks themselves that store the data).

- On a tape the magnetic material is in lines along the length of the tape.

A read/write head:

- This creates a magnetic field over the location on the disk/tape and magnetises the individual dots of magnetic material in binary patterns, storing the data. The electric current that flows through the head will jump between two values causing the two binary values (1 or 0) to be magnetised on the media.

An actuator:

- The read/write head has to be moved over the location on a disk, or the tape has to be wound through, so the location is under the static head.

- Imagine a record player where the disk spins and the needle is moved in and out on an arm to reach each part of the record. This is how a disk drive works; the read head is on the end of an arm that is moved across the spinning disk.

- A tape drive moves the tape to the heads rather than the head to the tape – just like a cassette tape in a stereo.

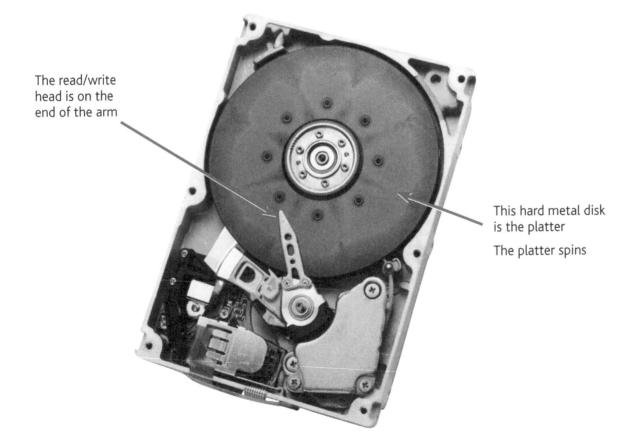

The read/write head is on the end of the arm

This hard metal disk is the platter

The platter spins

Optical storage media

The word "optical" should make you think about the eye and how we see the world in terms of reflected light. Optical media work in a similar way. Lasers write data to the disk and read data from it. Optical media include CDs and DVDs.

OPTICAL STORAGE DEVICES		
	CD	DVD
Cost	Very cheap 50 CD-R for £12 (24p each)	Very cheap 50 x 4.7GB DVD-R for £15 (30p each)
Capacity	640MB	4-17GB
Access Speed	Up to 7.6 MB/s (52x)	16 MB/s (12x)
	Much slower than magnetic hard disk	
Portability	Easy to carry in a large pocket or bag	Easy to carry in a large pocket or bag
Durability	Depends on how it is stored. Quality degrades over time, life expectancy of a CD-R about 20 to 100 years but can start degrading in 18 months!	Recordings last 2-15 years so not considered reliable for long term storage
Reliability	Good for medium term but degrades over time	
Typical use	CD-ROM for software distribution CD-R or CD-RW for backup/archive	Backup/archive where higher capacity is needed

How optical media work

A CD or DVD is read using a laser. If you looked at the surface of a CD under a microscope it would look like this:

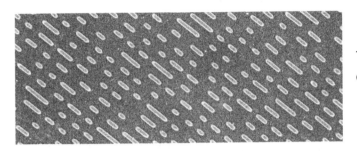

The magnified surface of a CD-ROM.

- Data is stored on CD-R, CD-RW, DVD-R & DVD-RW using pits and lands

- A laser changes a dye layer on the disk so that it is either opaque (pit) or transparent (land)

- A laser shines on the disk and light is reflected back from the dye layer in different ways depending on whether it is opaque or transparent

- Because a surface can be reflective or not, it is easy to store 0 and 1 as reflected or not reflected

- With CD-RW and DVD-RW it is reversible, but with CD-R and DVD-R it is not

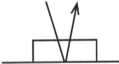

This is the slowest of all storage media.

A CD-ROM, which might contain a game for example, is created at the factory so that you can only read it. In this case, the silver layer in the disk is permanently marked.

Solid state/flash storage media

If you need to move work from school to your home PC you might use a USB Memory Stick (sometimes called pen drives). These use a newer technology called flash memory. It is solid-state memory, which just means that it does not have any moving parts. This makes the access speed of flash memory very high (but not as fast as RAM) and there is less to go wrong. Flash memory is a type of RAM but will not replace the type of RAM used in the main memory as its access speed is too low. It is however, an excellent replacement for a hard disk in devices like notebooks and tablet PC. With no moving parts it is more robust and uses less power. This type of memory is also used in mobile phones, tablet PCs and cameras.

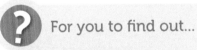
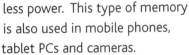

? For you to find out...

How much storage/memory there is on a modern camera?

How do hard disks and CD ROMs work?

FLASH STORAGE DEVICES		
	Internal Solid State/ Flash Storage	**USB Memory Stick**	**Memory Card**
Cost	128GB for £65 750GB for £330	32GB for £15 128GB for £35	64GB SD card £29
Capacity	128 to 750GB	64MB to 256GB	128 MB to 64GB
Access Speed	6Gb/s *(faster than magnetic disk because no moving parts)*	480Mb/s *(speed of USB2 interface)*	*Dependent on type of card and device interface*
Portability	Not portable, built into PC	Very small, can put in any pocket or on a key-ring	Very small, designed for portable devices
Durability	More robust than hard disks with moving parts. Said to be 5-10 times more durable than a hard disk drive	Very durable – often survive washing machine! Some can be snapped quite easily	Very durable - not sensitive to temperature or knocks
Reliability	Extremely reliable	Very reliable but can corrupt files if removed from PC too soon	Very reliable
Typical use	Notebooks, tablets, slim laptops	Personal use, moving files between computers	In phones and cameras

How solid state media work

Flash memory is a type of chip called an **EEPROM**, which stands for **Electronically Erasable Programmable Read-Only Memory**. It is essentially a huge grid of transistors, each of which can be set to the value 1 or 0. The transistors are set to 1 or 0 by passing electrical current through the EEPROM but once they have been set they will stay like that until they are reset to another value. Imagine turning a row of light switches on and off – it takes energy to move the switch but it stays like that until you move it again later.

Storage media capacity compared

The following chart shows common storage media and their relative sizes.

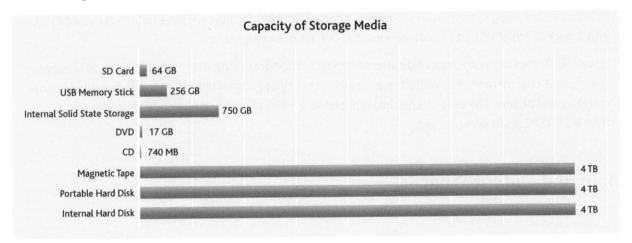

Capacity of Storage Media

Media	Capacity
SD Card	64 GB
USB Memory Stick	256 GB
Internal Solid State Storage	750 GB
DVD	17 GB
CD	740 MB
Magnetic Tape	4 TB
Portable Hard Disk	4 TB
Internal Hard Disk	4 TB

Note:

Details in the above tables and graph may already be out of date (written August 2014). You should research products that are currently on the market to see how quickly technology advances.

Hardware Developments

The AQA specification says that students should:

- be able to discuss how developments in different hardware technologies (including memory and processor) are leading to exciting innovative products being created, e.g. in the mobile and gaming industries

Computer technology changes very quickly so you should keep in touch with current changes by reading magazines and websites that are up to date. Memory technologies are changing in several ways so consider how these factors affect the products coming into shops now. These factors include:

- **Capacity and density:** You can now buy a 64 GB SD card for a camera where a few years ago a 4 GB card was considered high capacity. Increasing capacity in itself isn't the challenge; you could just add more cards. The ability to increase the capacity on the same size card is the challenge. Higher density means devices can store more without getting bigger, or devices can store the same amount but get smaller. You only have to look at mobile phones to see how these have become smaller and lighter and yet can still store more music and even video. The capacity of primary memory has also improved so computers can run more applications at the same time and complex games can run easily on a "basic" computer.

- **Speed:** Although flash memory is still much slower than RAM it is significantly faster than a magnetic hard disk. This means that bulky and sensitive hard disks can be replaced with smaller, lighter, faster and more reliable flash memory. Computers start up more quickly, as this is dependent on how long it takes to load the operating system from secondary storage into RAM. So now we have notebooks you can slip into a pocket, tablet PCs and smart-phones that behave like computers.

- **Price:** Flash memory is cheaper and easier to produce so devices using flash memory become cheaper as well. Lower cost memory has led to the increased capacity of gadgets like MP3 players, hand-held game consoles and phones. The cost of RAM has dropped so a £500 PC today has more RAM and more storage than a £500 PC just two years ago.

Input and Output Devices

The AQA specification says that students should:

- be able to categorise devices as input or output depending on their function

This book does not attempt to describe the full range of devices currently available. There are many websites that comprehensively describe how these work. It is however important to understand what input and output devices exist and how to choose appropriate devices for a situation.

Input devices

We live in an analogue world of continuously changing variables. In order to process or store data we must somehow capture it and convert it into a digital representation. *Chapter 4: Data Representation*, describes how we store text, numbers, sound, images and instructions on a computer. Here we are concerned with the devices that will capture the inputs.

Keyboard: Used for data entry into computers. This is a full keyboard with function keys and a number pad but laptops and other devices may have cut-down versions of this. Pressing a key generates a character code which is sent to the computer.

Mouse: Used for pointing at objects on the screen and selecting items by clicking or double-clicking. Right-click usually brings up a context-sensitive menu. A scroll wheel between the buttons makes it easy to move up and down the screen. Connected to the computer by a wire and USB connector or wirelessly, the mouse detects movements and position either with a ball or a reflected light source under the mouse. A variation on the mouse is a trackerball where the user moves a larger ball on the top surface instead.

Touch screen: Used on phones and tablet PCs as well as applications such as help screens in banks and tourist information offices. Instead of using a mouse you can just touch the icons to select them. On some devices moving two fingers apart or together on the screen zooms in or out and tapping icons is equivalent to a double-click.

Barcode scanner: A laser scans the barcode on a product to detect the width of the black and white stripes. This generates the product number so the rest of the details can be found in a database.

OMR: Optical Mark Recognition is used for multiple-choice tests, evaluation forms and lottery tickets, for example. This uses a light source that reflects a different amount of light back from shaded boxes to detect the data for input.

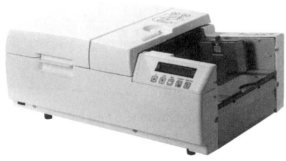

OCR: Similar to OMR but this is Optical Character Recognition. The software interprets the marks as characters and generates text and some formatting detail which is transferred to a file or document for further word processing.

Joystick: Although mention of a joystick probably makes you think of a game controller, joysticks do have other uses! They are used to control wheelchairs and to remotely control lights, security cameras and bomb-disposal robots. The game controller's cross-shaped control pad is a type of joystick.

Microphone: used to input sound that can either be recorded in a file or processed by voice recognition software for other uses. Voice recognition could be used for many applications such as hands-free phone dialing, controlling devices in a house if you are not mobile, a karaoke game or for security identification.

Sensors: These measure temperature, light levels, pressure, humidity and many other physical properties in the real world. These can then trigger processes and the appropriate output action as required. For example, if a thermistor (temperature sensor) reading is higher than 23°C, the computer could signal motors to open the greenhouse windows (see "actuators" under Output Devices in this chapter). The sensor shown is an Xbox movement sensor.

Sensors are also used to track eye movement or head movement to allow disabled people to use computers. Eye and head movements operate a pointer on the screen, instead of using a mouse.

Specialised keyboards: There are many variations on the keyboard and touch-screen that allow people with various disabilities to operate a computer. Features may include: bigger keys, specialised layouts for different purposes, braille overlays and brighter colours for contrast.

Foot-operated mouse: This works in the same way as a normal mouse, complete with left- and right-click buttons. It is designed to be easily operated with a foot instead.

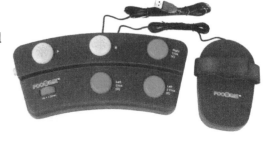

Camera: A camera can be used as a web-cam so you can see the person you are phoning over the internet but it can also be a way of communicating with the computer if you do not have the use of your hands. Instead of using a mouse a disabled person can control an on-screen keyboard with eye or head movements detected with a camera.

Sip-and-puff switches: These are activated by the user's breath. A "puff" into the device might be the equivalent of a mouse click and a "sip" (or suck) might be the equivalent of holding a key down. This would be used with an on-screen keyboard.

? For you to find out...

Use **www.howstuffworks.com** to find out how these devices work.

Output Devices

Computer systems create many outputs for us. These can be printed reports, data on a screen, sound, pictures or an action that needs performing via a motorised control. Here are some output devices you may come across:

CRT monitor: CRT stands for Cathode Ray Tube. These are the heavy, old-fashioned monitors that take up a lot of space on the desk. Very few people use these now but in places like factories they are still used because the glass screen is more robust than a TFT screen.

TFT monitor: TFT stands for Thin Film Transistor. This type of screen is the thin screen you probably have at home or on a laptop. This is a variation on LCD technology. LCD stands for Liquid Crystal Display, the earlier version of TFT screens. These screens take up less space but are more easily damaged than a CRT monitor.

Speakers: To output sound the computer must synthesize sound from the digital file and output sound waves through speakers. These might be small speakers integrated into the computer, phone or other device, or they may be stand-alone speakers that attach to the computer by a headphone jack, for example. Headphones are a type of speaker.

Inkjet printer: This is probably the type of printer you have at home. It works by spraying ink onto the page so if you have big shaded areas on a page the page will come out a bit damp and wrinkled. For normal text they produce good quality printing at a low cost. The ink is never sealed on the page so if you use a highlighter pen on notes from an inkjet the ink will smudge. They are also quite slow so they are not suitable for a large office or classroom.

Laser printer: This is the type of printer you probably have in the classroom as it is quicker and quieter than an inkjet. The ink is in the form of a toner powder that is sealed onto the page by heated rollers. That is why your printed pages come out warm. The ink goes onto the page dry so the quality is much better and it won't smudge. These are more expensive printers and the toner cartridges are more expensive than inkjet cartridges, though you will get more prints.

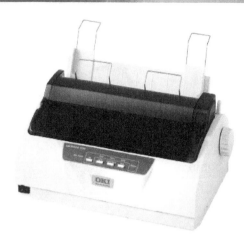

Dot-matrix printer: Before inkjet and laser printers we had dot-matrix printers. They worked a bit like a typewriter as a print head has to strike the paper through an ink ribbon to print text on a page. A dot matrix printer is termed an impact printer for this reason. They are still used today where companies have to use multi-part stationery. A laser printer would only print on the top page but an impact printer pushes through several layers that have carbon paper in between each sheet of paper. The paper is fed through the printer using the holes at the side. The holes are then torn off to give a printed page.

Braille printer: An impact printer that creates raised dots to represent each letter to allow blind people to read.

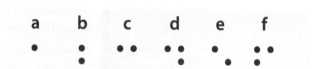

Actuator: The actuator is the device that performs some sort of mechanical action based on inputs. For example, a voice sensor might trigger a motor to close the curtains. Often these are used with sensors but they can also be used with touch screens. Modern aircraft use many sensors to provide input to computers that control the flight. Actuators move the flaps on the wings and the tail automatically.

Lights (LEDs): Lights are used to show that Caps Lock is on, that the computer is in standby or that a laptop is connected to the mains. Light-Emitting Diodes (LEDs) are used to output different signals to the user.

Is it an input or output device?

Sometimes a device is not just input or output. A touch-screen on a phone allows the user to input commands by tapping icons and also input text with an on-screen keyboard. A touch-screen is also an output device, displaying information for the phone user.

Another area of confusion is a camera. A digital camera these days is a complex device. It has a viewing screen that may also be a touch screen, as well as its own storage. So is a camera an input device? Well, a webcam on a PC is clearly an input device. A normal digital camera is really a computer system in its own right. When you plug it into your computer on a USB port you are looking at the secondary storage on the camera and transferring the pictures from one folder to another. At this point the camera is essentially just storage, as if you've plugged in a memory stick. If the camera is taking a picture then it is an input device getting real world analogue data and storing it as digital pixels.

In an exam you need to consider the context and use of any device to decide if it is an input, output or storage device.

Glossary of Terms

Central Processing Unit

CPU	The central processing unit that contains the processor, main memory and cache.
Main Memory/RAM	Also known as Immediate Access Store and Primary Memory The memory in the CPU that is used to temporarily store programs while they are running and the data used by these programs. The processor fetches instructions from main memory. Memory is made up of many addressable locations.
Processor	The component in the computer that fetches, decodes and executes instructions.
Cache	High speed memory in the CPU that is used to store a copy of frequently used instructions and data. Faster access speed than main memory. Used to improve CPU performance.
Clock Speed	Measured in Hertz or cycles per second, the clock speed defines how many instructions per second the processor can execute. The higher the clock speed, the faster the CPU can operate.
Level 1 Cache	Cache that is on the processor chip
Level 2/3 Cache	Cache that is on the motherboard, not on the processor. NB: More recent processors have L2 cache on the processor as well; in this case the cache on the motherboard is called Level 3 Cache
System Buses	The circuits/internal wiring that connect together the components within the CPU (e.g. processor and main memory).
Fetch-Execute Cycle	The process by which a program is run: instructions are stored in main memory, fetched by the processor one at a time, decoded and executed.
Dual-Core/Quad-Core	A CPU that contains multiple processing components (cores) that can operate independently to process more than one task at a time.

Memory

RAM	Random Access Memory: a type of memory that is read-write and volatile. Used for main memory.
ROM	Read-Only Memory: memory that is hard-coded at the time of manufacture. Stores the startup programs, called the bootstrap loader.
Bootstrap Loader	The first program that is loaded into main memory from ROM when a computer is switched on. This will load the operating system from secondary storage.
Volatile	Describes memory that loses its contents when the power is turned off, e.g. main memory
Non-Volatile	Describes memory that does not lose its contents when the power is turned off, e.g. hard disk.
Secondary Memory	Long term, non-volatile storage media such as hard disks, memory sticks, magnetic tapes and CDs.
Virtual Memory	Part of the hard disk that is configured to behave as an extension to main memory.
Magnetic Media	Secondary storage such as hard disks and tapes.
Optical Media	Secondary storage such as CDs and DVDs that is read using lasers.
Solid State / Flash Memory	Secondary storage that has no moving parts. Used in memory sticks, cameras and phones.
Pen Drive	Another term for a USB memory stick
EEPROM	Electronically Erasable Programmable Read-Only Memory. A chip made up of a grid of transistors, each of which can be set to the value 1 or 0. The type of memory used in flash memory.

Sample Questions

These questions are similar to the ones you may see in the exam. Good answers to these, along with exam hints and tips, can be found at the end of the book.

1 (a) What does ROM stand for?

(b) What is the difference between RAM and ROM?

(c) State the purpose of ROM in a computer system. [3]

2 (a) Jo's computer has 4 GB of RAM.

Describe two uses of RAM in a computer. [2]

(b) The computer uses virtual memory in addition to RAM.

(i) Explain what is meant by virtual memory, and why it is needed. [3]

(ii) Explain how virtual memory is used. [2]

(c) Jo finds that his computer runs rather slowly when he has several programs open. He has been advised to add another 4GB of memory.

Explain why this would help to improve the performance of his computer. [2]

(d) Explain how one other component of a computer's CPU that could be upgraded to improve the computer's overall performance. [2]

3 What is secondary storage? Give an example. [2]

4 **(a)** A student prepares a presentation on her home computer and has to take the file into school to present it in the lesson.

State two types of secondary storage the student may have used and describe how each would be used. [4]

(b) For the following secondary storage devices, pick its likely capacity from this list.

Use one of the following values in each row: 4 TB   256 GB   16 GB   700 MB [4]

	Capacity
CD	
DVD ROM	
Hard disk	
USB memory stick	

5 Describe the effects of developments in computer processors and memory on the products that we can buy.

The quality of written communication will be assessed in this question. [6]

Chapter 3: Data Representation

This topic is all about how data is stored in a computer. In this chapter you will learn how computers store numbers, text, images, sounds and program instructions.

Units

The AQA specification says that students should:

- understand the terms bit, nibble, byte, kilobyte, megabyte, gigabyte and terabyte

- understand that computers use the binary alphabet to represent all data and instructions

Computers are made up of complicated hardware that stores and processes data. If you break a computer down into its most basic components you have millions of circuits that either allow electricity to flow, or not. Imagine a whole row of light switches that you can switch on and off in different combinations to mean different things. Each switch is either on or off. It only has two states, which can be represented by 1 or 0. This is called **binary**.

A single **1** or **0** is a **b**inary dig**it**, or a **bit** for short. A group of eight bits is called a **byte**. Imagine you've taken a small bite out of an apple, you might call that a nibble. So four bits, half a byte, is called a **nibble**!

Just as a kilometre is 1000 meters, we can group together 1024 bytes to make a **kilobyte**.

8 bits	=	1 **byte**
1024 bytes	=	1 **kilobyte**
1024 kilobytes	=	1 **megabyte**
1024 megabytes	=	1 **gigabyte**
1024 gigabytes	=	1 **terabyte**

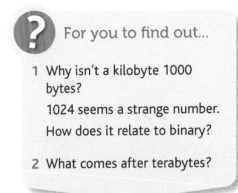

? For you to find out...

1 Why isn't a kilobyte 1000 bytes?
   1024 seems a strange number. How does it relate to binary?

2 What comes after terabytes?

Integers

The AQA specification says that students should:

- understand how binary can be used to represent positive whole numbers (up to 255)

Imagine you are back in primary school, learning to add again. 7+5 = 12, so you write down the 2 units but carry the group of 10. 23 would be 2 groups of 10 and 3 units.

Counting in binary is the same except instead of digits 0 to 9 we only have two digits, 0 and 1, so we carry the group of 2. In maths we call this Base 2. This is how we count to 10 in binary:

denary	binary	
0	0	
1	1	
2	10	Notice that we now go to the second column – one group of 2, no units
3	11	One group of 2 plus one unit 2+1=3
4	100	Now we go to the third column, 2 groups of previous column, so this is 4
5	101	
6	110	
7	111	
8	1000	Every time we go to the next column it is two times the previous column
9	1001	
10	1010	

Can you see the pattern? The column headings in a binary number double each time:

	x 2		x 2		x 2		x 2		x 2		x 2		x 2	

128	64	32	16	8	4	2	1
2x2x2x2x2x2x2	2x2x2x2x2x2	2x2x2x2x2	2x2x2x2	2x2x2	2x2	2	1
2^7	2^6	2^5	2^4	2^3	2^2	2^1	1^0

To convert the binary number `111001` into a denary (decimal or base 10) number use the column headings. The number below is `32+16+8+1 = 57` (add up the column headings where there is a 1).

128	64	32	16	8	4	2	1
0	0	1	1	1	0	0	1

To convert a denary number to a binary number, use the column headings. You need to find the biggest column heading that you can take away from the number and start there:

Let's convert 57 into binary:

The biggest column heading we can take out of 57 is 32 (the next one is 64, which is too big).

Write a 1 under column heading 32. That leaves us with 57 − 32 = 25.

Write a 1 under column heading 16 (because we can take 16 out of 25). 25 − 16 = 9

You should be able to see now that 9 is an 8 and a 1 so we end up with:

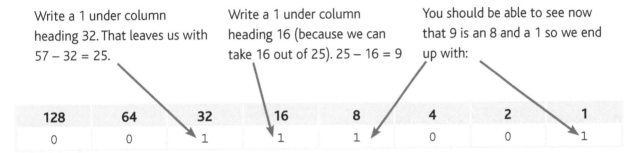

128	64	32	16	8	4	2	1
0	0	1	1	1	0	0	1

Always double check by adding the columns up at the end. They should give you the number you started with! `32+16+8+1 = 57`✓

Here are some more examples:

Denary	Binary							
	128	64	32	16	8	4	2	1
23	0	0	0	1	0	1	1	1
84	0	1	0	1	0	1	0	0
255	1	1	1	1	1	1	1	1

So far we have only looked at numbers using eight columns. This is an 8-bit number, or a byte.

`00000011` is binary for 3 but so is `11`. You do not need the leading zeros for it to be a valid number but we tend to write groups of 8 bits because computers usually store data in bytes.

Obviously numbers can be bigger than 255 but in computers we need to represent data in a specific number of bits. For example, in some programming languages an integer is stored in 16 bits (2 bytes) whereas a real number is stored in 4 bytes.

At GCSE level you will only need to work with 8-bit numbers.

 For your information...

255 is a significant number in binary; it will come up a lot in other parts of the course!

What do you notice about the number 255 in binary?

Hexadecimal Numbers

> **The AQA specification says that students should:**
>
> - understand why hexadecimal number representation is often used and know how to convert between binary, denary and hexadecimal

Which of these is easier to remember: **01011011** or **5B**? Humans are not very good at remembering long strings of numbers so, to make it easier, we can represent every group of 4 bits (a nibble) with a single digit.

The smallest value you can have with 4 bits is 0000. The largest value is 1111. This means that we need to represent the denary values 0 to 15 with a single digit. The trouble is, we only have numerical digits 0 to 9, so to get around this problem we use letters to represent the digits 10, 11, 12, 13, 14 and 15.

This is called Base 16 in maths, or **hexadecimal** in computing. We abbreviate this to **hex**.

This is how we count to 16 in denary, binary and hex:

denary	binary	Hex
0	0	0
1	1	1
2	10	2
3	11	3
4	100	4
5	101	5
6	110	6
7	111	7
8	1000	8
9	1001	9
10	1010	A
11	1011	B
12	1100	C
13	1101	D
14	1110	E
15	1111	F
16	10000	10
255	1111 1111	FF

> **?** For you to find out...
>
> How is hex used to code colours in HTML (web pages)? For example, what colour is #FF00FF?
>
> Search on "Colour palette hex" and see what you can find out.

A single hex digit replaces 4 bits.

15 is the biggest number you can have with 4 bits so 16 is one group of 16 and no units (just like we did before with binary).

255 is 15 groups of 16 + 15 units i.e. (15 x 16) + 15

To Convert a Binary Number to Hex:

In GCSE Computer Science you will only need to work with 8-bit binary numbers, which can be represented as two hex digits. The first hex digit represents groups of 16, the second hex digit represents the units.

The denary number 92 =   0101   1100   = 5C in hex

                       5   12   *(12 is replaced by C)*

    (groups of 16) *(units)*

To Convert a Denary Number to Hex:

To convert the denary number 182 into hex the first step is to work out how many groups of 16 there are in 182. Secondly work out how many units are left over.

        182 / 16 = 11 remainder 6

        11 is B in hex. 6 is just 6   So   182 denary = B6 hex

Alternatively, you can convert the denary to binary first and then convert the binary to hex, as above.

Real Numbers

> ### The AQA specification says that students should:
>
> - understand that a binary code could represent different types of data such as ....
>   real number

Real numbers are numbers with fractional parts such as 234.46, 0.00034 or 3.0. These can be very big or very small so we need to store them differently from integers. We don't need to store all the zeros, just the main part of the number (called the **mantissa**) and how many times we need to multiply it by 10 (called the **exponent**).

Real numbers are stored using floating point. Here are some examples in decimal:

Real number written long-hand	In floating point notation	What we need to store
2,300,000,000.00	23×10^8	mantissa = 23 exponent = 8
0.000000000345	345×10^{-12}	mantissa = 345 exponent = 12

At GCSE level you are not required to do this in binary; you will learn how to convert fractions, negative numbers and floating point numbers to binary in the A Level course.

Dates

The AQA specification says that students should:

• understand that a binary code could represent different types of data such as .... date

Although dates look like three numbers (24/10/1978) they cannot be simply stored as three integers. In order to process dates the computer needs to be able to calculate that 02/09/2011 is 5 days after 28/08/2011. Dates have to be stored in a logical sequence so they can be processed usefully.

Different computer systems and programming languages store different ranges of dates and time. To explain the basic principal, let's consider this example:

• Our system is going to store dates between 01/01/0001 and 31/12/9999.

  - This is the earliest and latest date using our standard notation of dd/mm/yyyy.

• Assuming an average of 365 days per year and 9999 years we have about 365 x 9999 (3,649,635) different dates that all need to be stored.

• Each date needs to be stored as a unique number:

  - 01/01/0001 = 1

  - 02/01/0001 = 2

  - and so on

• If we needed 8 bits to store 256 different numbers (see earlier binary section) then to store the numbers 1 to 3,649,635 we will need a lot more bits!

Some programming languages use 4 bytes (32 bits) or 8 bytes (64 bits) to store dates. Some systems use as many as 32 bytes to store the date and time as one data item.

For you to work out...

Write a program to calculate the number corresponding to today's date.

Assume 01/01/0001 is numbered 1 and remember to factor in leap year.

Characters

The AQA specification says that students should:

- understand how characters are represented in binary and be familiar with ASCII and its limitations

Every time a character is typed on a keyboard, a code number is transmitted to the computer. The code numbers are stored in binary. Different sets of codes are available for different types of computer. PCs use a **character set** called **ASCII**, American Standard Code for Information Interchange. A character set is the group of characters that can be coded.

A character set is the group of symbols that a computer can represent and includes letters, digits, punctuation marks and control characters. Control characters are things like **Esc** and **Enter** (aka **CR** because it used to be called Carriage Return).

The next page shows a version of ASCII that uses 7 bits to code each character. The biggest number you can have with seven bits is 1111111 in binary (127 in denary). The smallest number you can have with seven bits is 0000000 (0 in denary). This means that you can have 128 different characters in the character set (using codes 0 to 127).

Notice that the characters are in numerical sequence:

A	065
B	066
C	067
D	068
E	069

If "A" is 65 then "C" must be 67.

Also notice that the uppercase letters come before the lowercase letters so you can say that "A" <"a". (In a sorted list, "Andrew" will appear before "above", for example.)

In order to encode all the possible global character sets in binary, for example Japanese, Russian or Greek characters, many more bits are required to represent each character, so there are alternative encoding systems.

Other character encoding systems include:

- **Unicode:** An encoding system that typically has 16 or 32 bits per character so can code 2^{16} (65,536) or 2^{32} (4,294,967,296) different characters in its character set.

- **EBCDIC** (*pronounced eb-sid-ic*): Extended Binary Coded Decimal Interchange Code, an 8-bit encoding system that has 2^8 (256) different characters in its character set.

7-bit ASCII Table

ASCII	DEC	Binary	ASCII	DEC	Binary	ASCII	DEC	Binary	ASCII	DEC	Binary
NULL	000	000 0000	space	032	010 0000	@	064	100 0000	`	096	110 0000
SOH	001	000 0001	!	033	010 0001	A	065	100 0001	a	097	110 0001
STX	002	000 0010	"	034	010 0010	B	066	100 0010	b	098	110 0010
ETX	003	000 0011	#	035	010 0011	C	067	100 0011	c	099	110 0011
EOT	004	000 0100	$	036	010 0100	D	068	100 0100	d	100	110 0100
ENQ	005	000 0101	%	037	010 0101	E	069	100 0101	e	101	110 0101
ACK	006	000 0110	&	038	010 0110	F	070	100 0110	f	102	110 0110
BEL	007	000 0111	'	039	010 0111	G	071	100 0111	g	103	110 0111
BS	008	000 1000	(	040	010 1000	H	072	100 1000	h	104	110 1000
HT	009	000 1001	)	041	010 1001	I	073	100 1001	i	105	110 1001
LF	010	000 1010	*	042	010 1010	J	074	100 1010	j	106	110 1010
VT	011	000 1011	+	043	010 1011	K	075	100 1011	k	107	110 1011
FF	012	000 1100	,	044	010 1100	L	076	100 1100	l	108	110 1100
CR	013	000 1101	-	045	010 1101	M	077	100 1101	m	109	110 1101
SO	014	000 1110	.	046	010 1110	N	078	100 1110	n	110	110 1110
SI	015	000 1111	/	047	010 1111	O	079	100 1111	o	111	110 1111
DLE	016	001 0000	0	048	011 0000	P	080	101 0000	p	112	111 0000
DC1	017	001 0001	1	049	011 0001	Q	081	101 0001	q	113	111 0001
DC2	018	001 0010	2	050	011 0010	R	082	101 0010	r	114	111 0010
DC3	019	001 0011	3	051	011 0011	S	083	101 0011	s	115	111 0011
DC4	020	001 0100	4	052	011 0100	T	084	101 0100	t	116	111 0100
NAK	021	001 0101	5	053	011 0101	U	085	101 0101	u	117	111 0101
SYN	022	001 0110	6	054	011 0110	V	086	101 0110	v	118	111 0110
ETB	023	001 0111	7	055	011 0111	W	087	101 0111	w	119	111 0111
CAN	024	001 1000	8	056	011 1000	X	088	101 1000	x	120	111 1000
EM	025	001 1001	9	057	011 1001	Y	089	101 1001	y	121	111 1001
SUB	026	001 1010	:	058	011 1010	Z	090	101 1010	z	122	111 1010
ESC	027	001 1011	;	059	011 1011	[	091	101 1011	{	123	111 1011
FS	028	001 1100	<	060	011 1100	\	092	101 1100	|	124	111 1100
GS	029	001 1101	=	061	011 1101	]	093	101 1101	}	125	111 1101
RS	030	001 1110	>	062	011 1110	^	094	101 1110	~	126	111 1110
US	031	001 1111	?	063	011 1111	_	095	101 1111	DEL	127	111 1111

Images

The AQA specification says that students should:

- understand how bitmap images can be represented in binary

Images can be stored in different ways on a computer. A drawing that you create in PowerPoint is a **vector** graphic. It is made up of lines and shapes with specific properties such as line style, line colour, fill colour, start point and end point. The computer stores all of this data about each shape in binary.

When you take a photograph on a digital camera, the image is not made up of individual shapes. The picture somehow has to capture the continuously changing set of colours and shades that make up the real-life view. To store this type of image on a computer the image is broken down into very small elements called **pixels**. A pixel (short for picture element) is one specific colour. The whole image may be, for example, 600 pixels wide by 400 pixels deep. 600 x 400 is referred to as the picture's **resolution**. If the resolution of a picture is increased, then more pixels will need to be stored. This increases the size of the image file.

Making an image file

10	10	10	10	10	10	10	10
10	00	10	00	10	00	10	10
10	10	00	00	00	10	10	10
10	00	00	01	00	00	10	10
10	10	00	00	00	10	10	10
10	00	10	00	11	00	10	10
10	10	10	10	11	10	10	10
10	10	10	10	10	11	10	10
10	11	11	11	10	11	11	10
10	10	11	11	11	11	10	10
10	10	10	10	11	10	10	10

This image of a flower uses 4 colours. Therefore 2 bits are needed to record the colour of each pixel:

11	10	01	00

The number of bits used to store each pixel dictates how many colours an image can contain. 8 bits per pixel will give 256 possible colours. The number of bits per pixel is referred to as the **colour depth**.

If the colour depth is increased so more bits are used to represent each pixel, then the overall size of the file will increase.

If we record the value of each pixel in this image, starting from the top left-hand corner and going left to right across each row, we end up with the following data file:

```
10  10  10  10  10  10  10  10  10  00  10  00  10  00  10  10  10  10  00
00  00  10  10  10  10  00  00  01  00  00  10  10  10  10  00  00  00  10
10  10  10  00  10  00  11  00  10  10  10  10  10  11  10  10  10      etc
```

For the computer to interpret this file and rebuild the picture it must know some other things about the data file; for example, that the picture's resolution is 8x11 pixels and the colour depth is 2 bits per pixel. Data about the data file itself is called **metadata**.

Sound

Sound waves are **analogue**, which means continuously changing. Anything stored on a computer has to be stored in a **digital** format as a series of binary numbers. To store sound on a computer we need to convert the waveform into a numerical representation. The device that takes real-world analogue signals and converts them to a digital representation is called an Analogue-to-Digital Converter (**ADC**).

For sound waves, the analogue signal is converted as follows:

- Analogue sound is received by a microphone

- This is converted into an electrical analogue signal

- The signal amplitude (height of wave) is measured at regular intervals (sampling)

- These values are rounded to a level (quantisation)

- The values of these levels are stored as a series of binary numbers in a file

01	0.8
02	2.0
03	3.4
04	4.8
05	6.3
06	8.1
07	10.0
08	12.0
09	14.0
10	16.0
11	17.4
12	18.0
13	17.8
14	17.2
15	15.8
16	13.8
17	11.3
18	8.4
19	5.3
20	3.0
21	1.7
22	1.0
23	1.2
24	2.0
25	3.3
26	5.0
27	7.0
28	9.0
29	11.0
30	12.0

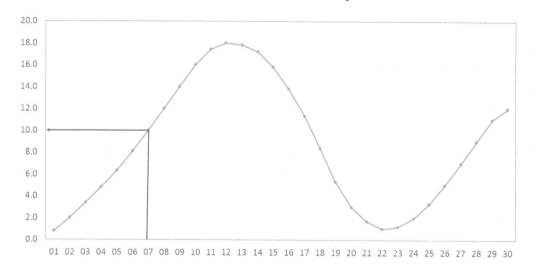

Sound Quality is affected by:

- **Sample Resolution:** The number of bits used to store each sample.
  The more bits that are used, the better the accuracy of the sound file. In the graph of a sound wave above, the sample resolution on the Y axis is shown in denary to 1 decimal place. It could be more accurately represented with 2 or more decimal places. The same holds true in binary.

- **Sample Interval:** The time period between taking samples/measurements.
  The more frequently the sound is sampled, the better the quality of playback. In the graph above, samples are taken every 1 unit of time – if we halved the sample interval, the wave would be more accurately represented.

Data or Information?

The AQA specification says that students should:

• understand what is meant by the terms data and information

All data on a computer is stored in binary. Real-world information needs to be stored in some way. Letters of the alphabet are stored as ASCII codes in binary, numbers are stored as binary representations in floating point, pictures are stored as a series of colour codes per pixel etc.

The computer will interpret the binary data based on its context. A .jpg file storing an image, for example, will also contain **metadata** that indicates what sort of file it is and how the binary digits are to be interpreted. When a program such as Paint opens an image file it will present the data from the file as a picture on the screen, not as a series of numbers. It converts the raw data into information – in this case, an image.

Data can also be described as the raw facts and figures. Information is how we present data so that it is useful or meaningful to the reader. Information is often defined as processed data that has meaning and context.

For example, here is some information about student progress:

Name	Data Rep Test /35		Hardware Test /50		Database Test /20		Average Score
Sam	20	57%	45	90%	12	60%	69%
Ellie	34	97&	35	70%	20	100%	89%
Josh	23	66%	41	82%	17	85%	78%

It is information because the way it is presented makes it clear what it means. It has context and meaning. If information is processed data, then conversely, data is coded information.

If we consider input and output on a computer system we can then say:

• Input devices take real-world inputs and convert them to (digital) binary code numbers, **data**

• **Data** is stored, not information

• Output devices take **data** from a computer and present it as **information** to the user

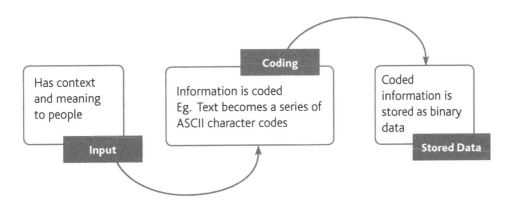

Glossary of Terms

Units

Bit	A single binary digit: 1 or 0
Byte	8 bits
Nibble	4 bits
Kilobyte	1024 bytes / 2^{10} bytes
Megabyte	1024 kilobytes / 2^{20} bytes
Gigabyte	1024 megabytes / 2^{30} bytes
Terabyte	1024 gigabytes / 2^{40} bytes

Numbers

Binary	Base 2 number system, used by computers, uses the digits 1 & 0 only.
Denary	Base 10 number system, how we normally count, uses digits 0 to 9.
Hexadecimal (hex)	Base 16 number system used by humans to represent groups of four bits at a time. Uses digits 0 to 9 and A, B, C, D, E, F.

Characters

Character set	The set of symbols that can be represented by a computer. The symbols are called characters and can be letters, digits, space, punctuation marks and some control characters such as "Escape". Each character is represented by a numerical code that is stored as a binary integer.
ASCII	American Standard Code for Information Interchange: a 7-bit character set used by PCs. (There is also an extended ASCII character set that uses 8 bits.)
EBCDIC (pr. eb-sid-ic)	Extended Binary Coded Decimal Interchange Code: an 8-bit character set used by older mainframes.
Unicode	A 16-or 32-bit character set that allows many more characters to be coded.

Images

Bitmap Image	An image that has been stored as a series of values per pixel. The colour of each individual pixel is stored in a file.
Pixel	Short for picture element. It is the smallest component of a bitmapped image.
Colour Depth	The number of bits used to represent the colour of a single pixel in a bitmapped image. Higher colour depth gives a broader range of distinct colours. For example, an image stored as a .gif file uses 8 bits per pixel so the image could use 256 different colours.
Resolution	The number of pixels in an image expressed as: the-number-of-pixels-across x the-number-of-pixels-down e.g. 400 x 600.
Metadata	Data about data. In the case of image files metadata is the data the computer needs to interpret the image data in the file, for example: resolution, colour depth and image dimensions.

Sound

Analogue	A continuously changing wave such as natural sound.
Digital	Data that is made up of separate values. How data is stored on a computer.
Sample Rate	The number of times per second that the sound wave is measured. The higher the rate the more accurately the sound wave is represented.
Sample Interval	The time gap between measurements of the sound wave being taken. Another way of expressing the sampling rate.
Sample Resolution	The number of bits used to store the value of each sample. The greater the number of bits the more accurately the value is stored.
ADC	Analogue to Digital converter: takes real-world analogue data and converts it to a binary representation that can be stored on a computer.

Data and Information

Data	Facts and figures with no context or format to give them meaning. Coded information.
Information	Processed data that has context and format so that it conveys meaning.

Sample Questions

These questions are similar to the ones you may see in the exam. Good answers to these, along with exam hints and tips, can be found at the end of the book.

1 (a) State the denary representation of the binary number 10110110. [1]

(b) State the hexadecimal representation of the denary number 137.

You must show your working. [2]

(c) State the denary representation of the hexadecimal number 2C.

You must show your working. [2]

(d) Give one reason why error codes are often displayed on the screen in hexadecimal, instead of binary. [1]

2 State the number of bytes in a megabyte. [1]

3 The ASCII code for "A" is 1000001

(a) What is the total number of characters that can be encoded in ASCII? [1]

(b) State the binary code for "D". [1]

4 Describe how a sound wave received by a microphone is converted into a sound file on the computer. [3]

5 Describe the effect on a bitmap image file of increasing the picture's resolution. Why does it have this effect? [2]

Chapter 4: Software Development Life Cycle

This topic is all about the steps involved in the creation of a software system from the moment the idea is conceived to finally delivering a complete solution and then maintaining it until a new system is required. This process is referred to as the software development life cycle.

Software Development Life Cycle

The AQA specification says that students should:

- understand the software development life cycle

- be able to explain what commonly occurs at each stage of the software development life cycle

- be able to identify at which stage of the software development life cycle a given step would occur

Developing a complex piece of software can take months or even years. The purpose of the software development life cycle is to break it down into smaller steps to make the process manageable. The goal of this process is always the same: to produce a piece of software that meets the users' needs, is produced within budget and is finished on time.

The next section looks at the key stages in any software development life cycle. Typically each stage involves certain key activities and produces outputs that are used in the next stage.

The stages in the software development life cycle

The development of a new computer system has a number of well-defined stages:

- Feasibility study

- Analysis

- Design

- Implementation

- Evaluation

- Maintenance

Each of these stages is described in the following paragraphs.

Feasibility study

In the case of a major new system, a feasibility study will be carried out. The aim of this is to understand the problem and to determine whether it is worth proceeding. Factors to consider include:

- whether the technology exists to do what is required

- how much the system will cost; will it cost more to develop than money saved or increased income generated over the next few years?

- whether there are any legal issues that need to be considered – for example, would the new system infringe the patents or copyright of another company?

- what will the consequences be of the new system: how it will affect people working in the organisation which has requested the system, and those outside the organisation who may be affected by it

- how long it will take to develop

Analysis

The systems analyst is the person who carries out this stage, which involves gathering information about what the current procedures are and what the new system will need to do. There are several ways in which the analyst can do this:

- **Interview** people who will use the software or will be involved with the system in some way

- Use **questionnaires** to get input from larger groups of people

- **Observe** how people currently work (they may not tell you everything you need to know)

- Get examples of **existing documentation** that will give us an insight into what the data look like

Having collected information about the existing system (if there is one), and the requirements of the new system, the analyst will produce a written report, often called the **Specification** or **User Requirement**.

This defines what the software must do but doesn't say anything about how it will do it (that is covered in the Design). The specification is important because it is used to create the design. It is also the document that the finished product will be compared against in the Evaluation stage.

Having collected lots of data about the new system we need to analyse it. In this stage a developer would draw diagrams that identify processes and show how data flows around the system (you do not need to know about Data Flow Diagrams at GCSE but you will probably use them at A Level). They would also look at the data itself. A **data dictionary** is used to capture what each data item looks like (data item name, data type, any formatting needed, any restrictions on range etc.)

Here is an example of part of a Data Dictionary:

Data Item	Type	Format	Validation
Surname	string	Capitals	< 25 characters
Shoe Size	integer	-	Between 3 and 15
DoB	date	dd/mm/yyyy	Between 01/01/1900 and today

You might find a data dictionary a useful planning tool in your controlled assessments to capture what variables you plan to use.

The output from the Analysis stage will be the Specification or User Requirement. This defines what the software must do but doesn't say anything about how it will do it (that is covered in the Design). The specification is really important because it is used to create the design. It is also the document that the finished product will be compared against (in the Evaluation stage).

Design

The software design will include:

- **a description of the data** used in the system: its data type, format and any validation to be carried out when the data is entered. It will also include any file structures or database tables that need to be defined.

- **input** screens/user interface

- **output** screens and reports

- **a description of how data flows through the system:** system flowcharts may be used to show the different parts of the system and how data flows between them. For example, in a sales order processing system there may be several sub-tasks involved; fulfil the order, decrease the number of items in stock, invoice the customer, send them a catalogue in a few weeks' time, enter customer payments and so on.

- **how the data is processed:** The system will be split up into different modules, each performing a specific task. Flowcharts or pseudocode may be used to describe the algorithms used in each module.

- **how the software will be tested:** typically a formal test plan will be drawn up at the design stage to make sure the software is tested objectively.

Implementation

Implementation includes the following activities:

- **Coding and testing** the software (more on testing later in this chapter)

- **Writing documentation:** technical documentation, for whoever has to support and maintain the software later, and a user guide

- **Installing the software** for the user

Evaluation

Having completed the software, the customer will want to be sure that it does everything it was supposed to do. The developer will be keen to prove that it does so he can get paid! The software must be evaluated against the original Specification/User Requirement document. This is also called **Acceptance Testing**.

Maintenance

The final stage of the software development life cycle is to maintain the software while it is in use. The software may be in use for years with no issues but there are three reasons why it may need maintaining:

CAP

- No matter how well a system is tested, real users using real data will often find problems that didn't occur in testing. Fixing bugs is called **Corrective Maintenance**.

- The users' requirements change so the software needs updating to meet the new requirements. This is called **Adaptive Maintenance** because the existing software is being adapted to meet a new need.

- Even though the software meets the user requirements in terms of functionality, the users may request performance improvements or changes in how it looks that make it easier to use. This is called **Perfective Maintenance**.

Corrective, Adaptive, Perfective

Think of a maintenance person in a CAP!

Commonly Used Lifecycle Models

The AQA specification says that students should:

- understand that there are several lifecycle models that can be used (e.g. cyclical, waterfall, spiral)

- be able to discuss the advantages and disadvantages of these lifecycle models

There are several approaches to performing the stages described above. These are standard approaches used in industry to develop software so they are known as models. We will consider four models in the next few pages, each with its own benefits and disadvantages.

Waterfall model

The **Waterfall Model** defines definite steps that are completed one at a time to guide the process from beginning to end. Each step has specific outputs that lead into the next step. You can return to a previous stage if necessary but you then have to work back down through the following stages. The user/customer is involved at the start of the process, in the Analysis stage, but then has little input until the Evaluation stage. This model was adopted from the manufacturing industry, where changes to hardware made later in the project had high cost implications to work already completed so it was important to get each stage right before moving to the next. Although still popular, it has been superceded by more effective models now.

Feasibility Study

Analysis

Design

Implementation

Evaluation

Maintenance

There are variations on this basic diagram: for example the stages could be labelled Feasibility Study, Analysis, Design, Coding and Testing, Installation, Evaluation, Maintenance.

Advantages:

- Self-contained steps are easy to manage

- Defined processes and outputs per step

- Good model for managing large groups of developers working in parallel

Disadvantages:

- Requirement changes mean going back to an earlier stage that had already been completed

- Changes can be costly in money and time

- Lack of customer involvement after Analysis means issues are not highlighted until the Evaluation

Cyclical model

In the Waterfall Model the emphasis is on completing each stage as well as possible and then progressing to the next stage until the software is finished. Although you can go back to previous stages if you have to, the waterfall is essentially a one-off, linear development plan. The **Cyclical Model** shown in the diagram to the right still works through the stages in order but acknowledges that after maintaining a system for a while, there are likely to be new requirements, which take the software's life cycle back to the start. Consider a product like MS Windows. As soon as one version is released and evaluated, new ideas for the next version are being suggested and checked out. That takes the product's life cycle back into a new Feasibility Study, ready to go through the whole cycle again.

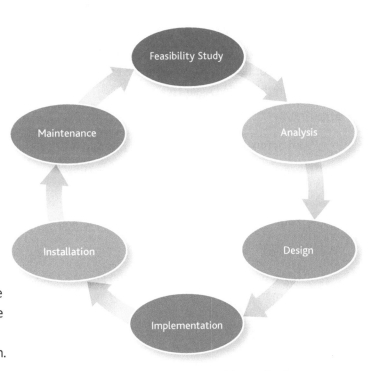

Advantages and disadvantages are essentially the same as the Waterfall model. One additional advantage is that the final stage, Maintenance, logically starts the next cycle of the process so it maps better on to the real life cycle of a complex piece of software.

Spiral model

The **Spiral Model** uses the same structured steps but introduces the idea of developing the software in iterative (repeating) stages. At the start of the process the requirements are defined and the developers work towards an initial prototype. Each successive loop around the spiral generates a refined prototype until the product is finished. Each time around the spiral the following activities are performed:

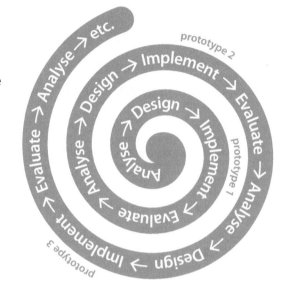

- **Analyse** the requirements for the next prototype

- **Design** the next version, the new prototype

- **Implement** (code and test) the new prototype

- **Evaluate** the new prototype, which generates a plan for the next iteration

At the end of each loop around the spiral a new, more refined prototype is produced until an operational version of the software is ready. The Spiral Model is mostly used for large scale projects, for example, projects that take years to deliver. Smaller projects use a variation on this called Agile (see next).

Advantages:

- Well defined steps in the process make it easy to manage

- Interim prototypes highlight issues quickly so that the end product is more likely to be what the customer wants

- Iterative nature of the process means changes can be easily incorporated as feedback is received

Disadvantages:

- It takes time to build prototypes and get feedback, so it takes longer to get the product to the customer

- Longer timescale means it costs more to develop

Agile model

Agile is an iterative process just like the Spiral Model but it is heavily based on customer involvement throughout the process and makes use of small multitasking teams of developers. The process starts by creating a prototype, which the customer gives feedback on. This informs the changes to the prototype, which is then developed forward. At every stage the customer is involved and gives feedback as the prototype is developed into the full product.

The Agile method of developing software is best suited to small groups of developers who work together rather than large projects where developers work on separate parts in parallel. It is very popular in environments where requirements are changing rapidly, as developers using Agile can change the product as it develops.

The advantages of this model are essentially the same as the Spiral Model with the following addition:

- Small multitasking groups make the team flexible to changing requirements so this is more effective in a rapidly changing environment

The disadvantages of this model are essentially the same as the Spiral Model with the following addition:

- This way of working is only suitable for smaller development teams

Prototyping

The AQA specification says that students should:

- understand what prototyping is

- be able to discuss the advantages and disadvantages of using prototyping when developing solutions

- have experience of using prototyping to create solutions to simple problems

The Spiral Model and Agile Model of software development both use prototypes. A prototype is an approximation to the finished product, a model or sample, which is designed to show the customer/user certain aspects of the product being developed. This enables the user to comment at stages within the development life cycle having seen a sample, rather than just working from a list of requirements.

The advantages of this approach to working are:

- The customer can give feedback having seen or used the prototype so the feedback will be better

- The developer can get meaningful feedback before the product is developed too far

- The product can be changed based on feedback during the development rather than getting to the end and the customer saying "that's not what I meant!"

The disadvantages are:

- More costly to keep making prototypes

- More time-consuming having to get feedback at each stage

- The customer can keep moving the goal-posts, which may make the development timescales longer

Testing

Computer systems control many aspects of our lives. If software does not work properly the implications can vary from mild annoyance to widespread chaos and, in some cases, injury or fatality. It is important that the software is tested rigorously. This means using all of the possible types of data to simulate every situation it may be used in, not just using sensible data that should work, but all the daft things a user might do by mistake. Software should not crash because of something a user types; it should cope with invalid data in a sensible way such as giving an error message. The developer must systematically test different routes through the code and test with all different types of valid and invalid input data.

Types of testing

Once all or part of the program code has been written, developers will use different types of testing to make sure it works correctly:

Unit/module testing

A complex piece of software will be broken down into modules, which may be written by different programmers. Each unit or module will need to be tested on its own to make sure it does what it was supposed to do. Developers will use different types of testing to test their modules; for example, using trace tables before the code is written to test the logic of their algorithms. (This is discussed in *Chapter 7: Programming Concepts and Algorithms*.)

Integration testing

At some point, when all of the separate modules have been coded and tested, they will need to be brought together (integrated) in one system. In theory they should all have been designed to work together but each programmer may have made assumptions that affect how their module works with other parts of the system. It is important to test the whole system after the modules have been integrated.

Alpha testing (aka peer review)

Once the programmers have completed the software and it has been systematically tested, they will get other developers within the company to peer-review it. Developers are sometimes too close to the coding to see how well it really works. A colleague using the software with no expectations is more likely to use it in the same way as a real user. This may highlight areas that need improving or fixing.

Beta testing

If this is commercial software, the company may not want to launch the product to everyone straight away. They are more likely to do Beta testing first. Beta testing involves giving the software to a small group of potential customers so it can be tried out in the real world. For example, if you have developed a phone app, you may have tested it on three or four types of phone but real customers will try it out as it would be used on lots of different phones. Usually these customers get the software free or cheap in return for feedback.

Acceptance testing

If software has been developed for a specific customer based on their requirements, then they will want to do Acceptance Testing. The developer goes through a plan of agreed tests with the customer, to prove that the software does what was asked for. This is usually the point at which the developer can say they have completed the project and expect to get paid.

Creating a test plan

How do you know if your program really works? It may run and produce output but you need to check that the output is as expected. If you made a spreadsheet that multiplied pounds by a conversion rate to get dollars you would probably type in a number like 1 or 10 to see if the number of dollars looked right. Programs are tested in a similar way. Different test values are put into the program to test that the output is correct.

A good way of planning your testing is to write down the sample data that you will use and what results you expect to see with that input. This is a **Test Plan**. It is important that you think about this before you write the program so you don't move the goalposts later!

You can formalise your plan by using a table with the following headings:

Test purpose	Test data	Expected outcome	Actual outcome

The first three columns are part of the design and planning stage and the final column is completed when you test the finished program.

If numbers or dates are being entered by the user, then you should use test data that checks both ends of the allowed range (the **extremes**) as well as data that should not be allowed, just outside this range. This is known as testing **boundary data**.

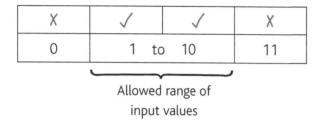

Allowed range of
input values

Note:

The term "extremes" doesn't mean extremely big or extremely small but refers to the extremes of the range, the smallest and largest values allowed.

The test plan for testing this validation would look like this:

Test purpose	Test data	Expected outcome
1 Check user can only enter numbers between 1 and 10	1 (lowest valid number)	Input is accepted
2 Check user can only enter numbers between 1 and 10	10 (highest valid number)	Input is accepted
3 Check user can only enter numbers between 1 and 10	0 (invalid number)	User gets an error message and is asked to enter number again
4 Check user can only enter numbers between 1 and 10	11 (invalid number)	User gets an error message and is asked to enter number again
5 Check user can only enter numbers between 1 and 10	5 (typical valid number)	Input is accepted
6 Check user can only enter numbers between 1 and 10	? (erroneous value)	User gets an error message and is asked to enter number again

Notice that we have ended up with six tests to test one validation rule because we have tested:

- **Valid data** entry values: anything between 1 and 10 in this case
- **Invalid data** entry values: still a number but not in the allowed range, breaks the rules
- **Erroneous data** entry: something that is not a number at all
- **Boundary data** entry: checking the extremes (1 and 10) and one value outside of the extremes (0 and 11)

If text is being entered, the test plan must check what happens when you enter nothing or a string that is too long, as well as the text you would expect to be ok.

Test purpose	Test data	Expected outcome
7 Check user password works	"Frogs" (valid data, correct password)	User allowed to continue
8 Check user password works	"cats" (valid data, but incorrect password)	Error message and asked to try again
9 Check user password works	" " (invalid data entry, no password)	Error message and asked to try again

In your controlled assessments you will probably do a similar test plan and then show the evidence from each test as a labelled screenshot. Just ticking the tests doesn't prove anything!

Glossary of Terms

Software Development Stages

Feasibility Study	The initial investigation of a problem to check that a solution is possible. This includes technical, economic, legal, operational and scheduling feasibility.
Analysis	Gathering data and analysing it to identify the system requirements. This stage generates the Requirements Specification.
Design	The detailed description of how the system will be created. Includes details of the inputs, outputs, processing algorithms and data structures, as well as the Test Plan.
Implementation	Coding, testing and installing the software, and writing documentation.
Evaluation	Checking that the software meets the Requirements Specification. Includes Acceptance Testing for software created for a specific customer.
Maintenance	Ensuring that the software continues to meet requirements as they change, fixing any bugs that are found and improving performance as required.
Corrective Maintenance	Fixing bugs in the software.
Adaptive Maintenance	Making changes to the software because the users' requirements have changed.
Perfective Maintenance	Improving the performance or usability of the software.

Software Development Models

Waterfall Model	A series of separate stages; each one is completed and provides inputs to the next. Although you can backtrack if issues are found, the model assumes forward movement from start to finish.
Cyclical Model	Structured stages as in the Waterfall Model but once the system is in Maintenance stage it generates new problems that lead back into the Feasibility Study and so on. Stages form a continuous cycle.
Spiral Model	Instead of doing each stage once, the Spiral Model has several iterations of the stages. Successive passes through the stages produce a more refined prototype until the system is complete.
Agile Model	Similar to a Spiral but the developers form small multitasking teams and the customer is involved at every stage.
Prototype	A simple version of the software that shows how it will look or behave. Intended as a sample or model to get feedback, which will move the development forward.

Testing

Unit/Module Testing	Testing an individual module of the software.
Integration Testing	Testing the modules together as an integrated system.
Alpha Testing	Peer Review of the software before release.
Beta Testing	Review of the software by sample customers who provide feedback on how the software performed in the real world.
Acceptance Testing	Formally testing the software with the customer to prove that it meets the Requirements Specification so the project is completed and the developer gets paid.
Test Plan	A formal set of tests designed to use all possible types of input and all paths through the program; designed to check that the output is as expected for specific types of input.
Valid Data	Data that should be allowed by the program. It conforms to the validation rules. For example, if a range of 1 to 10 is allowed, then valid data will be any number between 1 and 10 inclusive.
Invalid Data	Data that are of the right type but do not conform to the validation rules and should be rejected by the program. For example, if a range of 1 to 10 is allowed, then invalid data will include -251, 0, 11 and 345.
Erroneous Data	Data that is not the right type such as letters instead of numbers. Should be rejected.
Extreme Data	The data values at either end of the allowed range. For example, in a range of 1 to 10, the extreme values are 1 and 10.
Boundary Data	Data either side of the range limits. For example in a range of 1 to 10 boundary data will include 0, 1, 10 and 11.

Sample Questions

These questions are similar to the ones you may see in the exam. Good answers to these, along with exam hints and tips, can be found at the end of the book.

1 A programmer is developing a piece of software.
   The programmer uses **alpha testing** and **beta testing** as part of the development process.

   Compare these two types of testing. Your answer should include a description of each of these types of testing.

   In this question you will be marked on your ability to use good English, to organise information clearly and to use specialist vocabulary where appropriate.   [6]

2 Two years ago, a car hire company installed new software to manage all their bookings. They now need to perform maintenance on this software.

   Describe **three** different types of maintenance that the company might have to do and give an example of each category.   [6]

3 A supermarket wants to develop a new point of sale (checkout) and stock control system. As part of the Analysis stage of this development, a consultant must gather data about current systems and the requirements for the new one.

   List **three** methods that the consultant could use to collect data and describe how they could be used in this situation.   [6]

4 A programmer is designing the test plan for an online ordering application. One of the data entry boxes on the form is for the quantity required. The program should only allow the user to submit the form if the quantity is between 1 and 50.

   Complete the test plan below with tests for three **different** types of data that could be entered by the user. (Part of the first one has been done for you).   [7]

Test purpose	Test data	Expected outcome
Quantity text box accepts valid data		Data accepted

5 A programmer wants to develop a major piece of software.

   Two possible development models are the **waterfall** and **agile** models.
   Compare the advantages and the disadvantages of each model.

   In this question you will be marked on your ability to use good English, to organise information clearly and to use specialist vocabulary where appropriate.   [8]

Chapter 5: Networking

This topic looks at how and why we network computers; the client-server model of networking and how this is implemented in web-based applications.

Networking

The AQA specification says that students should:

- understand what a computer network is
- be able to discuss the advantages and disadvantages of using a computer network
- be able to describe and explain the bus, ring and star networking topologies
- be able to discuss the advantages and disadvantages of each of these topologies

A network is a collection of computers and peripherals connected together. We categorise networks as either Local Area Networks (LANs) or Wide Area Networks (WANs).

Local Area Network (LAN)

A **Local Area Network** is defined as a collection of computers and peripheral devices (such as printers) connected together within a single site. Notice that it is within a single site and not a single building. At school you probably have many different buildings within a campus. The school's LAN will connect computers together in all these buildings.

Consider how you work on a single laptop or PC at home that is not connected to a network. Compare this to how you work on computers at school, which are all on a LAN. A network in a large office building will provide all the same features that you have at school.

Wide Area Network (WAN)

A Wide Area Network, or WAN, is a collection of computers and networks over a geographically remote area.

The term "geographically remote" is a confusing one. It does not mean that networks have to be miles apart, although they may be. Geographical remoteness is more about what separates sites than the distance involved. However, the Internet is a WAN and is worldwide. At your school there will be a LAN that connects computers in various buildings. Your campus may be quite large but still connected in a LAN. If you have a split campus with a public highway or some other buildings in between the two campuses, then these will need to be connected in a WAN.

WANs use hired infrastructure to connect the LANs together; the school or business cannot install its own cables between the two sites. A business with offices in London, Leeds, Bristol and York will lease connections from a network service provider to connect the four office LANs together.

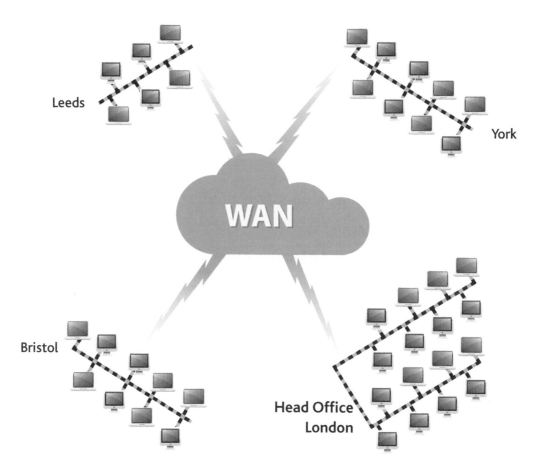

Benefits of Networking Computers

The benefits of networking the computers fall into these categories:

Sharing resources:

• Sharing folders and files so you can access files anywhere on the network from any computer and different people can access these files as needed

• Sharing peripheral devices such as printers and scanners

• Sharing an Internet connection

Communication:

• Using email to communicate with colleagues

• Using messaging systems to chat while you are working on other things

• Transferring files between computers

Centralised management:

• User profiles and security can all be managed centrally

• Software can be distributed across the network rather than having to install it on each individual computer

• Users can use any PC on the network but still see their own files

• Centralised backup of all files

Network topologies

Computers can be connected together in different layouts, or topologies. There are three basic topologies that are used but these may be combined in a large network.

Bus network

This is a topology only used in a LAN. Computers are connected to a single backbone cable. The computers all share this cable to transmit to each other but only one computer can transmit at any one time. This is fine most of the time if the network is not too busy but if there is a lot of traffic then transmissions interfere with each other and computers have to retransmit.

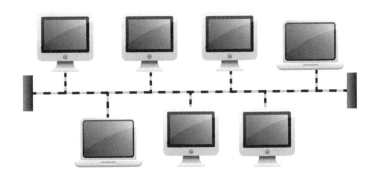

Advantages:	Disadvantages:
1 Easy and inexpensive to install – less cabling than in a star network	1 If the main cable fails then the whole network goes down
2 Easy to add new computers	2 Cable failures are hard to isolate because it affects all of the computers attached
3 Broadcasting onto a bus is faster than transmitting around a ring network through many devices	3 All data is broadcast on one cable so not secure
	4 Performance slows down as the amount of traffic increases

Ring network

Computers are connected to adjacent computers in a ring. Computers take it in turns to transmit, controlled by passing a token around the ring. Computers can only transmit when they have the token. This topology is only used for LANs and MANs (Metropolitan Area Networks). *(MANs are not part of this specification but worth looking up on the Internet - high speed fibre networks in campuses and cities)*

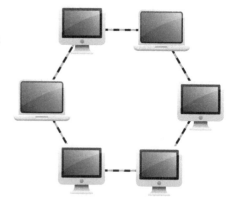

Advantages:	Disadvantages:
1 Not dependent on a central computer like the star network	1 A single node or link failure disrupts the entire network
2 Token-passing protocol is simple and therefore reliable	2 All connections shared so not secure
3 Consistent performance even when there is a lot of traffic	3 All data goes around whole network so slow

Star network

All of the computers have their own cable that connects them to a central switch or hub. The central computer controls the network. This is usually a switch or a server where shared resources are stored. This topology is used in LANs and WANs.

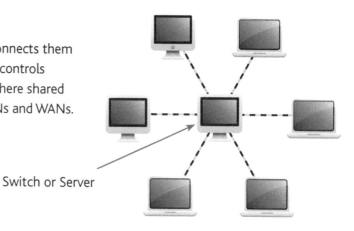

Switch or Server

Advantages:	Disadvantages:
1 If one cable fails only one station is affected rather than the whole network	1 Can be costly to install because there is a lot of cabling
2 Consistent performance even when the network is heavily used	2 If the central computer fails then the whole network goes down
3 Easy to add new computers	
4 More secure – messages are transmitted down links that aren't shared	

Client-Server Networks

The AQA specification says that students should:

- understand the client-server model

In your school you will be able to use your files on computers in different buildings. This is because they are not stored on the computer that you are using but are on a file server somewhere else in school. The **server** is a specialised computer with a different role from the normal PC. There will probably be a web server to host the school's external website and an email server. The email server receives all emails and distributes them to network users. It may detect and block incoming emails that it thinks are spam.

In a large network it is common to have shared files and resources on centralised servers. The computers that you use around school are referred to as **clients**.

In a client-server network:

- the network is centrally managed by a powerful computer called the server

- client computers communicate via a central server

- there are different types of server on the network: file server, email server, print server, web server

The client-server network approach is also used across a wide area network. For example:

- Your browser will act as a client to the web server, somewhere else in the world.

- Companies such as banks and supermarkets will have centralised databases, which are accessed across a WAN by applications on client PCs.

The client-server architecture is used over a WAN because the data is in one central place but is being accessed by a large number of client devices, which could potentially be anywhere in the world.

Client-server configuration

- *Client computers communicate via central server*
- *Files and email stored centrally*
- *Network managed centrally*

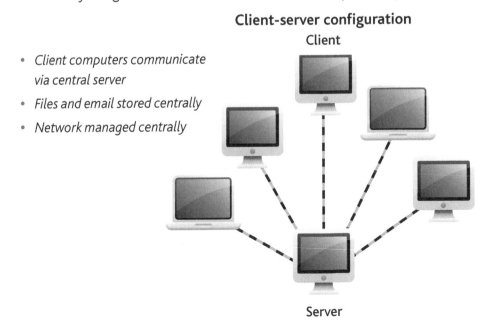

Client

Server

Coding for Client-Server Networks

> ### The AQA Specification says that you should be able to:
>
> • be able to explain how coding for a client-server model is different from coding for a stand-alone application

The basic principle of a client-server system is that the client requests data, the server processes the request and returns a response. Some examples of this would be:

• A browser (the client) requests a web page using HTTP
  The web server responds to the HTTP request by sending the requested page.

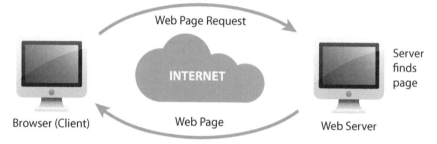

• MS Outlook on a client PC requests the contents of an email (user clicked "Open")
  The email server retrieves and sends back the message

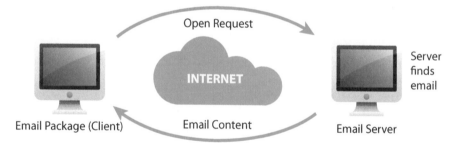

• A browser sends a request for product information using a form on a web page, which generates an SQL request to select certain records from the database. The web server processes the SQL request and returns the relevant product details

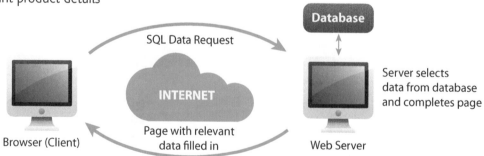

In client-server architectures there are two distinct parts to the coded solution with a network connection between them. Part of this solution will execute at the server and part at the client. This is very different from a standalone program where everything runs in one environment.

Some of the differences between a standalone application and a client-server application are:

- The programmer has to consider how to transfer the relevant data from the client to the server. In a standalone program there will be variables, which are stored on the local computer. In the client server scenario the values of variables may have to be sent to the server side for processing there. It is similar to passing parameters to a procedure except they are being passed across a network.

- The network connection between the client and server ends must also be taken into account when writing the program code. What happens if the connection is lost for a moment? Which end of the program is storing the data needed to restore the situation for the user? A client has a session with the server that must be managed in some way.

- The server software will need to respond to more than one client. A web server may have many clients requesting pages at the same time, many of them maybe requesting the same page. This means that the server software has to have a component that detects requests and puts them in some sort of queue, as well as a module that gets requests off the queue and processes them.

- The server cannot be turned off; it must always be available, waiting for requests. The client application can just be active when it is needed.

- A client-server application has to be modular in structure. The program parts that link to a database should be independent from the part that manages the network interface, for example. If the network connection changes then that part must be updated to handle a different protocol without having to rewrite the whole server end.

- On a standalone computer you have user access rights to run certain applications. A client server application is getting requests from across the network so, if the data requested is confidential, the server-end programming will need to include client authentication of some kind.

In summary:

Stand-Alone Applications:	Client-Server Applications:
All data stored locally (disk or main memory)	Data must be passed between the client and server
No network connection to manage	Must manage a network link and the associated sessions
Single user	Multiple clients per server so must manage a request queue
Used as needed, can be closed in between uses	Must be available all the time
Modular structure less important	Must be designed and created in a modular fashion
Local access rights on host PC is sufficient security	Clients have to be authenticated before data is sent to them

The Handshake Process in Networks

One aspect of client-server architecture is the way the two ends communicate over a network. To start a session between the client and server there is a communication sequence that takes place. This is called **handshaking**. In a human conversation, before we start to chat properly, we shake hands and introduce ourselves. Even informally, you get someone's attention ("Hey Fred…") and make sure they are listening before you tell them something ("… you've got to hear this! ……").

In TCP/IP (the protocol used to communicate over the Internet) there is a **three-way handshake** process that sets up communication between a client and a server. Once the three-way handshake has been successfully completed, a session is established between the devices and communication can take place.

The three steps are as follows:

1. The computer that is initiating the communication will send a synchronisation request, called a SYN, to the server.

2. The server sends the client's own SYN back to them with an acknowledgement that it has been received (an ACK).

3. The client acknowledges the servers response, which completes the session setup.

The client can now communicate with the server.

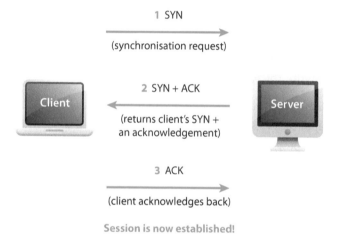

Web Application Concepts

In the previous section we looked generally at client-server principles. This section of the chapter looks specifically at a client-server web application, i.e. requesting and receiving a web page.

Client-server in web applications

You have probably made some web pages in school, perhaps using HTML or Dreamweaver. You may have just two pages linked together, with some information and pictures on them, perhaps with some hyperlinks to other sites or pages. Every time you open your pages, the content will be the same; it won't automatically update if some of the details have changed over time. When a page is hard-coded in this way (so that there are no parts that update automatically) it is called **static**.

When a company creates a website it won't hard-code all the product details into the pages because they change regularly. An Internet sales company such as Amazon or eBay has a basic page layout, which is then populated with the relevant product details, usually based on the customer's search criteria.

When you fill in a search box to look for "free books", this will form part of an SQL select statement to get the matching details from a database (see *Chapter 6: Databases* for details on how SQL works). These are called **dynamic** web pages and are updated from a database every time you request them. When your browser requests a page from the web server, the web server will fill in the dynamic parts at the server side and then send an up-to-date page to your computer (the client). For this reason database driven web-page programming is also referred to as server-side programming. This is different from the client-side programming, which is executed by the browser.

| Search | Kindle Store ▾ | Free books |

Client-side programming

Client-side programming is used for code that only affects the client's actual page at that moment in time, and doesn't need data from elsewhere. Client-side code is executed by the browser and may be used to:

- store data in cookies
- perform validation of data entry on forms
- create Flash animations and Java applets that run on a page
- display adverts when you hover over key words

Validation is when the computer software checks that the data entered is reasonable or sensible and conforms to rules about the type of data allowed, for example, checking that the user has filled in all the required data in an online form. If they miss out a key box that must be filled in then they should get an error message and be asked to fill in that data. This can all be done locally by the browser; there is no need to communicate with the central server.

There are several types of validation that are commonly used on data entry forms, which would be executed at the client end by the browser. However, not all validation checks can be done in isolation at the client-end. Some validation checks are done at the server end (see next section).

- **Range check:** a number or date is within a sensible/allowed range
- **Type check:** data is the right type such as an integer or a letter or text
- **Length check:** text entered is not too long or too short, for example: a password is greater than 8 characters, a product description is no longer than 25 characters
- **Presence check:** checks that some data has been entered, that it has not been left blank
- **Format check:** checks that the format is appropriate such as a postcode or email address

Validation can only check if data is reasonable. It cannot tell if it is correct. This is an important differentiation. If the "Student's Details" form prompts for Date of Birth the application can check that the data entered would be appropriate for that age group, it cannot tell if you enter November instead of December by mistake.

Whilst validation ensures that the data entered are sensible, **verification** double checks that it has been typed in correctly. This is where data is entered twice and the two versions are compared. If they are different the user can be prompted to try again. This is commonly used where email addresses and passwords are entered on forms.

As well as validation, client-side programming is used for:

- **Pop up adverts** that appear when you hover over keywords (so annoying!).

- **Cookies** are used to store data about how you use web pages. They store details that make it easier for you to use the page next time you go to that web site. For example, it might prompt you as you start to type a search or enter a username. Client-side programming stores data in cookies on your local PC.

- **Flash animations and Java applets** are code embedded in the webpage, which will run at the client-side when you view the page in your browser.

Server-side programming

Server-side programming is used for any processing that needs input from a centralised source such as a database of customers or products. Any data that is confidential in nature must be stored securely in a centralised place (says the Data Protection Act). Also, duplicating data leads to data inconsistency so companies want a single central data store (see *Chapter 6: Databases*).

Some of the activities that are processed at the server are:

- **Retrieving data from a database:** e.g. a bank customer wanting to see their latest statement or a customer searching for something on an online shopping site. Consider a search for a book on an online book site where you enter a book title.

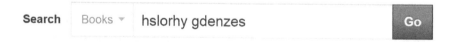

The web page will send the search criteria to the server where an SQL query will retrieve the relevant product details and populate the page. If the product doesn't exist, you will get a message saying that the product could not be found:

Your search **"hslorhy gdenzes"** did not match any products.

This is a result of server-side processing of the SQL search and checking if any records/rows have been found. The server-side programming will then populate the page with either the appropriate product details or a message saying it could not find any matches.

- **Populating a page with the latest details:** e.g. an exam board's website where all the latest papers can be seen by students.

- **Checking username and password** combinations to authenticate a customer on a site that requires membership: e.g. technical forums, gaming sites.

- **Some forms of validation** such as existence checks. As we said in the previous section, not all forms of data entry validation are done at the client. Some types of validation require communication with a central server. An **existence check** makes sure that a product or customer exists in the database, for example, if an order is being entered in a system it checks if that product actually exists in the database. This has to be processed at the server-side.

- **Counting how many people have visited a site.** Keeping count of how many people have visited a site must obviously be done at the server end. (However, the applet that displays a hit-counter on a page is client-side programming. You can download free applets to put on your own web pages.)

Creating Web Pages in HTML

The AQA specification says that students should:

- have experience of coding solutions to simple web application problems

Using the language you have been taught, you should have coded a simple web application so that you have some practical experience to complement this theory. You may need to use this in a controlled assessment.

This book does not attempt to teach you everything you need to know to create a web site but the following sections look at the basics of creating a static page in HTML, adding tables to structure data on the page and using some basic JavaScript to validate data entry on a form. In *Chapter 6: Databases* we consider how to populate these tables from a database.

Web pages are written in a programming language called **HTML**, HyperText Mark-up Language. HTML is used to describe the page content. It is used with a Cascading Style Sheet (**CSS**), which defines how the content is styled. Some styling can be coded with HTML but it is considered good practise to use CSS for styling and HTML for content.

> **!** See HTML and CSS in action...
>
> Check out this website to see how the same HTML content can look with different Cascading Style Sheets!
> *www.csszengarden.com*

```
<div class="summary" id="zen-summary" role="article">

    <p>A demonstration of what can be accomplished through <abbr
    title="Cascading Style Sheets">CSS</abbr>-based design. Select any style
    sheet from the list to load it into this page.</p>

<p>Download the example <a href="/examples/index" title="This page's
source HTML code, not to be modified.">html file</a> and <a href="/
examples/style.css" title="This page's sample CSS, the file you may
modify.">css file</a></p>

</div>
```

HTML is coded using **tags** that define the page structure. You can write HTML in a basic text editor and save the file as "filename.html". You can then run the page in your browser. Here is a very basic webpage in HTML:

```
<html>
  <head>
      <title>Seahorses in the UK</title>
  </head>

  <body>
      <h1> Dorset Wildlife </h1>
      <h2> Studland Bay Seahorses </h2>
      <p> Studland Bay is a breeding site for both spiny and short-nosed
      seahorses.</p>
      <h2> Habitat </h2>
      <p> The seabed in Studland Bay is mostly sandy with sea grasses
      and rocky outcrops, providing protection for the seahorses and
      hard surfaces for other inhabitants such as the native oyster
      to cling to.</p>
      <p>More on <a href=http://www.theseahorsetrust.org/seahorse-facts.
      aspx>
      seahorses</a> here.
      <br>
      <br>
      <img src="seahorse.jpg" width=640 height=360> </p>
  </body>
</html>
```

Tag	What it does
<head> </head>	Start and end tags for information *about* this page, not text that appears *on* the page.
<title> </title>	The text between these tags appears in the blue bar at the top of the browser window.
<body> </body>	The HTML between the body tags defines the page content.
<p> </p>	Paragraph tags that start and end a paragraph.
<h1> </h1> <h2> </h2>	Heading tags will go either end of heading text. The CSS will define how these look but normally heading text is bigger than normal page text.
<img>	The image source tag references a picture file and defines basic parameters such as size.
<a href...>	An href tag is a hyperlink reference that the following text will be linked to

The web page it produces looks like this:

Dorset Wildlife

Studland Bay Seahorses

Studland Bay is a breeding site for both spiny and short-nosed seahorses.

Habitat

The seabed in Studland Bay is mostly sandy with sea grasses and rocky outcrops, providing protection for the seahorses and hard surfaces for other inhabitants such as the native oyster to cling to.

More on seahorses here.

Writing a website using HTML would be time-consuming so there are application packages available to help design a website and create the HTML code for you. One example of this is Dreamweaver.

The page above is a **static** web page. This means that the content is hard-coded and does not change unless you edit the code for the page. This is quite restrictive, and most web sites will contain data that needs to be updated regularly or pages that interact with the user in some way. Pages that update automatically are called dynamic. This involves populating the web page from a database whenever the page is requested (see *Chapter 6: Databases* for details).

 Useful website…

An excellent site for details on HTML code is:
www.htmldog.com

Creating forms in HTML with client-end validation

Forms can be created in HTML, which will then need some validation code writing in a scripting language (e.g. JavaScript) to make sure the user types in sensible data and fills in all the boxes needed.

To illustrate the client-side validation code on an HTML page, here is a very basic form:

Subscribe to the Newsletter

If you would like to receive a copy of the newsletter then please complete the following details and click the button below.

Name

Email Address

Order newsletter now

The following code generates this form in HTML tags and the "Order newsletter now" button calls a JavaScript routine to check that both boxes have been filled in.

This form is called "Newsletter" and, assuming the result of this validation routine is "true", the web page called "Ordered" will be opened.

```
<body>

  <h1>Subscribe to the Newsletter</h1>

  <form name="Newsletter" method="post" action="Ordered.html">

  <p> If you would like to receive a copy of the newsletter then

      please complete the following details and click the button below.
    </p>

  <table width="50%" border="0">

    <tr>

      <td>Name</td>

      <td><input type="text" name="name" /></td>

    </tr>

    <tr>

      <td>Email Address</td>

      <td><input type="text" name="email" /></td>

    </tr>

    <tr>

      <td><input type="submit" name="Submit" value="Order newsletter
      now" onclick="return validateForm();" /></td>

    </tr>

  </table>

  </form>

</body>
```

This code creates text boxes for the user to type into. They have been put in a table to it looks nicer!

This code creates a submit button on the page. The "value" property is the text that appears on the button, the "onclick" property calls the JavaScript validation function, which is shown over the page

The following HTML code builds the form on the webpage and uses the following form tags:

Tag	What it does
<form ... > </form>	Start and end tags for the form area of the page. The opening tag includes properties such as the form's name and what action should happen next
<input type="submit" ... />	An input button, which has properties such as name and onclick. The onclick property calls a function, code that will be executed when the button is clicked
<input type="text" ... />	A text box for the user to type data into. It has a name property so it can be referred to in the validation code.

When the submit button is pressed the following code is called. This code is found in the <head> section of the HTML code and is enclosed within <script> tags to show where the scripting language starts and ends. This example uses JavaScript, which is one of the most popular scripting languages:

```
<script language="javascript" type="text/javascript">
    function validateForm() {
        var result = true;
        var msg="";
        if (document.Newsletter.name.value=="") {
            msg+="You must enter your name \n";
            result = false;
        }
        if (document.Newsletter.email.value=="") {
            msg+="You must enter an email address \n";
            result = false;
        }
        if(msg=="")  {
            return result;
        }
        {
            alert(msg)
            return result;
        }
    }
</script>
```

This tag marks the start of some code in a scripting language and states that this is JavaScript.

"result" is initialised to "True" but if either of the text boxes has been left empty it is set to False. This is the value that is returned to the form and will determine whether or not the next page is displayed.

This code checks if the text box is empty. If it is, an error message is added to the variable "msg" to build up a list of errors .....

...... which will be displayed as an alert box if the user hasn't completed the form.

Organising data on web pages with tables

Tables can be used on web pages to organise data in rows and columns. In this chapter we will just consider a static table with the data hard-coded into the page itself. In *Chapter 6: Databases*, we look at how these table tags can be used with server-side programming to present data from a database to create a dynamic web page (data is updated each time it loads).

Tables are useful to display rows of data in an organised manner. Tables consist of rows and columns and are created using the following tags:

Tag	What it does
<table> </table>	Starts and ends the table
<tr> </tr>	Starts and ends a table row
<td> </td>	Starts and ends a table data item (contents of one box in a table)

Here is a sample web page using a table to arrange static data:

```html
<html>
  <head>
    <title>Dinner menu</title>
    <style type="text/css" media="all">
        td { border: 1px solid #999;padding: 0.1em 1em;}
    </style>
  </head>
  <body>
    <h1> Leavers' dinner </h1>
    <table>
      <tr>
        <th>Course</th>
        <th>Menu</th>
      </tr>
      <tr>
        <td>Starter</td>
        <td>Grilled vegetable and mozzarella stack</td>
      </tr>
      <tr>
        <td>Main</td>
        <td>Beef Wellington with dauphinoise potatoes</td>
      </tr>
      <tr>
        <td>Dessert</td>
        <td>Lemon tart with raspberry coulis</td>
      </tr>
    </table>
  </body>
<html>
```

Leavers' dinner

Course	Menu
Starter	Grilled vegetable and mozzarella stack
Main	Beef Wellington with dauphinoise potatoes
Dessert	Lemon tart with raspberry coulis

Glossary of Terms

Networks

LAN	A collection of computers and peripherals connected together within a single site.
WAN	A collection of computers and LANs connected together over a geographically-remote area, using leased infrastructure.
Topology	A description of how devices are connected together. Does not necessarily represent physical layout.
Bus	A topology where each device is connected to a main cable, referred to as the bus. Any device can transmit at any time but only one transmission can occur on the main bus at any one time.
Ring	A topology where each device is connected to the next in a loop. Uses a token-passing protocol to manage transmission by one device at a time.
Star	A topology where each device has its own cable connecting it to a central device, which can be a switch or a server.
Client-server	A method of organising devices in a network where some computers have specialised roles: servers. The servers provide resources and services to the other computers, known as clients. Management of the network and shared resources/ files is centralised at the server.
Protocol	A set of rules that defines how devices communicate. Eg: IP, HTTP, HTTPS

Web applications

Handshake	The communication between a client and server device that initiates communication.
Three-Way Handshake	The TCP/IP handshaking process that consists of three exchanges: client sends a SYN to the server, server returns the SYN with an ACK, client sends an ACK.
TCP/IP	The protocol used between devices on the Internet.
Server-EndProgramming	Code that is executed at the server side of a client-server system. Usually coded in ASP or PHP.
Client-End Programming	Code that is executed by the browser at the client side of a client-server system. Likely to be coded in JavaScript or VB script.
Validation	When the computer software checks that data entered by the user is sensible and conforms to any defined rules.
Cookies	Text stored on the client computer, used by web sites to store data that makes the pages more user-friendly.
Applets	Small client-end programs that are embedded in web pages.
HTML	Hypertext Markup Language: the code that defines the content and structure of a web page.
CSS	Cascading Style Sheet: the code that defines how components within a page will be styled.
Static Web Page	The contents of the page are all coded into the page itself. The page does not have any content that automatically updates.
Dynamic Web Page	A web page that is populated from a database so its contents are always current.

Sample Questions

These questions are similar to the ones you may see in the exam. Good answers to these, along with exam hints and tips, can be found at the end of the book.

1 (a) Explain, with reasons, two advantages of using a star topology in a computer network.   [4]

   (b) State what is meant by the term "protocol" and give an example of one commonly used in networks   [2]

   (c) Describe the steps involved in handshaking in a network.   [3]

   (d) For each of the following events statements associated with a client-server network, indicate whether it is true or false by ticking one column in each row.   [4]

	Event	True	False
(i)	Querying a database is a server-side program		
(ii)	Validation only happens on the client-side		
(iii)	The browser runs on a client		
(iv)	Java applets are embedded in the server-side code		

2 Sam has been asked to write an online ordering system for a local bakery based on the client-server model. Describe how coding a client-server system differs from a standalone system by using this scenario as an example.

   In this question you will be marked on your ability to use good English, to organise information clearly and to use specialist vocabulary where appropriate.   [6]

3 An equipment hire company is expanding. At the moment their computers are all standalone but they are considering networking them. They plan to use a client-server model for their network.

   (a) State three benefits of networking the standalone computers.   [3]

   (b) Explain what is meant by a client in this network.   [2]

   (c) Explain the roles of servers in this network.   [4]

Chapter 6: Databases

This topic looks at the basic concept of a database, the key features and benefits of using a relational database and the basic theory behind relational databases such as Microsoft Access. Using Microsoft Access is a good way to get practical experience of relational database concepts and the screen shots in this chapter are from MS Access. This chapter does not provide instruction on how to use any one database package but provides an overview of the theory required for the GCSE exam.

Database Concepts

The AQA Specification says that you should be able to:

- understand the basic concepts of a relational database as a data store

Many organisations keep large amounts of data. A company stores data about its customers and staff, schools store data about the students, supermarkets store data about stock levels and customer buying patterns. This data could be stored in books, card files or spreadsheets, depending on the volume and type of data. When there are large quantities of data an organisation is most likely to use a database.

A **database** is described as a "structured collection of data". Clearly lots of data are being stored in a database but a database is more than just a store of data. A graphics file or collection of post-it notes on a wall is a "collection of data". A database has the data organised, or structured, into records. A school database, for example, will hold one record for each student.

 Note:

Data is a plural term so "...data are..." is not a grammar mistake! The singular is "datum", but this is seldom used so you will often see "data is..."

Traditional approach to data storage

In the past, before we had relational databases, the traditional approach to storing data in a company was for everyone to store their own data in their own files, probably using a spreadsheet or file of some sort.

A company might have a Sales department dealing with customers, an Accounts department that dealt with the same customers when they bought things and a Training department that trained the same customers on the products they'd just bought. Traditionally all of these departments kept their own data files, rather than sharing one file of data.

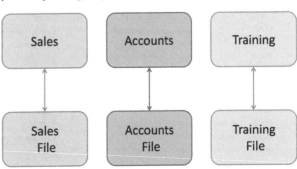

The problem with this approach is that there are three copies of the same customer details. When a customer moves house he phones the sales person and assumes that the rest of company now has his new address. In practice, the Sales department had the up-to-date details but the rest of company didn't. This is called "data inconsistency" and is the main problem with duplicating data in more than one place. This is easily solved by everyone sharing one database instead of using their own files.

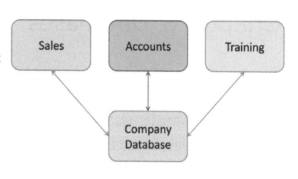

In computer systems we always try to avoid duplicating data in more than one place. So remember:

Data duplication leads to data inconsistency

Another issue that leads to data duplication (aka data redundancy) is the complex nature of the data being stored. Let's look at another example.

The spreadsheet below stores student details. Every student belongs to a tutor group. Notice that all of the details about Mrs Robson's tutor group are repeated for every student in her tutor group. This is known as a flat-file database and, as we said earlier, the duplicated data can lead to data inconsistency. If Mrs Robson's tutor group moves rooms, then several students' records would need to be updated. It is easy to miss one and end up with inconsistent data.

	A	B	C	D	E	F	G	H	I	J	K	L	M
1	Candidate Number	Name	Surname	Address1	Address2	Town	County	Postcode	Tutor Group	TutorName	Type	Room	
2	0001	Fred	Smith	23 The Road		Basingstoke	Hampshire	RG22 3FG	SJR	Mrs Robson	6th Form	203	
3	0002	Sally	Jones	32 Pleasant Str		Basingstoke	Hampshire	RG23 4SD	SLH	Miss Hickson	Year 9	120	
4	0003	George	Dotts	345 Boundary		Reading	Berkshire	RG1 4CV	SLH	Miss Hickson	Year 10	121	
5	0004	Joyce	Handel	2 Pickle Avenu		Reading	Berkshire	RG2 8NM	SJR	Mrs Robson	6th Form	203	
6	0005	Mabel	Pickles	The Old Post O		Guildford	Surrey	GU8 5GT	SJR	Mrs Robson	6th Form	203	
7	0006	Harry	Simpson	45 Foundary R		Basingstoke	Hampshire	RG24 6YU	PJT	Mr Thompson	Year 11	123	
8	0007	Xander	Erikson	Flat 3	Box Row	Reading	Berkshire	RG3 2SD	SLH	Miss Hickson	Year 10	121	
9	0008	Arnold	Holland	45 Reading Ro		Guildford	Surrey	GU1 5TY	PJT	Mr Thompson	Year 11	123	
10	0009	Lester	Jakes	567 Tower Stre		Basingstoke	Hampshire	RG23 4WQ	JKS	Mr Patel	Year 10	011	
11	0010	Jasmin	Flood	3a The Cottage	Dover Street	Basingstoke	Hampshire	RG24 7BN	JKS	Mr Patel	Year 11	012	

In computing we aim to store each piece of data just once. Ideally we should separate the data stored about tutor groups and the data stored about students. We only need to know which tutor group each student is in. We can refer to the other table to find out more details of that tutor group.

	A	B	C	D	E	F	G	H	I
1	Candidate Number	Name	Surname	Address1	Address2	Town	County	Postcode	Tutor Group
2	0001	Fred	Smith	23 The Road		Basingstoke	Hampshire	RG22 3FG	SJR
3	0002	Sally	Jones	32 Pleasant Str		Basingstoke	Hampshire	RG23 4SD	SLH
4	0003	George	Dotts	345 Boundary		Reading	Berkshire	RG1 4CV	SLH
5	0004	Joyce	Handel	2 Pickle Avenu		Reading	Berkshire	RG2 8NM	SJR
6	0005	Mabel	Pickles	The Old Post O		Guildford	Surrey	GU8 5GT	SJR
7	0006	Harry	Simpson	45 Foundary R		Basingstoke	Hampshire	RG24 6Y	
8	0007	Xander	Erikson	Flat 3	Box Row	Reading	Berkshire	RG3 2SD	
9	0008	Arnold	Holland	45 Reading Ro		Guildford	Surrey	GU1 5T	
10	0009	Lester	Jakes	567 Tower Stre		Basingstoke	Hampshire	RG23 4V	
11	0010	Jasmin	Flood	3a The Cottage	Dover Street	Basingstoke	Hampshire	RG24 7B	

	K	L	M	N
	TutorGroup	TutorName	Type	Room
	SJR	Mrs Robson	6th Form	203
	SLH	Miss Hickson	Year 9	120
	PJT	Mr Thompson	Year 11	123
	JKS	Mr Patel	Year 10	011

A spreadsheet is fine for storing small amounts of data but a large company would have thousands of records and a much more complex set of data to store. On the previous page we split the data into two logical groups, student details and tutor group details but once you've done that, a spreadsheet is not the most appropriate way of storing these data. It does not create the necessary links between the two tables; we need to use a **relational database** instead.

A relational database stores the data in tables, just like we created in the spreadsheet and it works on the principle of storing data just once. It creates separate tables of data that are related (linked together by a common field) which means that no data is duplicated unnecessarily.

Reducing data duplication (data redundancy) has several benefits:

- reduces the risk of data inconsistency
- makes maintaining the database much easier
- reduces the size of the database

To understand relational databases there is no substitute for making one yourself. Use Microsoft Access or another database package to create your own relational database. The following sections look at the basic theory.

Relational Databases

The AQA specification says that students should:

- be able to explain the terms record, field, table, query, primary key, relationship, index and search criteria

A relational database is a collection of data stored in related tables. In the spreadsheet example in the previous section we split the one big spreadsheet table into two tables, one about students and one about tutor groups.

In a relational database we create a table for each entity (a person, object or event) that we want to store data about, so a **table** is "a collection of data about a specific entity". We use a database package, such as Microsoft Access, to create these tables and to create logical links or **relationships** between them.

Here is the spreadsheet example from earlier in the chapter, recreated as tables in Access. There are two entities, student and tutor group, so we create a table for each. This avoids storing the same data twice (avoids redundancy). Notice that the tutor group initials appear against each student so we know which tutor group they are in. This same field also appears in the tblTutorGroup table so we can then reference the tutor group details. These fields have a special function in the database; they are used to create a **relationship** between the two tables.

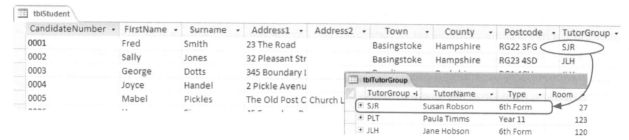

Fred Smith is in tutor group "JLH". This field connects tblStudent to tblTutorGroup so the tutor group details can be accessed. From the two related tables we can see that Fred Smith goes to classroom 27 for tutor time.

Each table contains records for each student or each tutor group. The records are made up of fields, individual data items such as "Surname" or "Town". With potentially hundreds or thousands of records it is critical that the computer can tell which one is which so every record must have a unique identifier. The field that uniquely identifies each record in a table is called the **primary key**.

The primary key can be a number or text but every record must have a different value for this field. In the example above the primary key for the Student table is "CandidateNumber". The primary key for the TutorGroup table is "TutorGroup" (the tutor's initials in this case).

In Access, the relationship between the two tables appears like this:

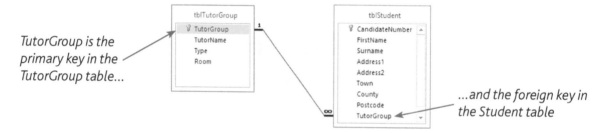

TutorGroup is the primary key in the TutorGroup table...

...and the foreign key in the Student table

It shows the two tables and the fields they contain. It shows the primary key fields in each table with the key symbol. It also shows the relationship created between the two tables. Be aware that you can only create a relationship from the primary key in one table to the same field in the related table. The field used is called the **foreign key**.

Records and fields

Each table in our database has data stored as records and fields. A table stores data about an entity; for example we have a Student table that stores data about students. Within this table each specific student (an instance of student) has lots of data items stored about them. Each data item is a **field** and these fields collectively form a **record**.

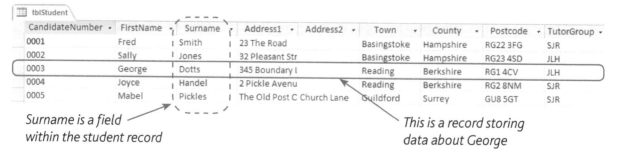

Surname is a field within the student record

This is a record storing data about George

Using queries to interrogate the database

Stored data is only as useful as what you do with it. Once data has been stored in a database the users need to be able to find out things about it and generate reports.

In databases you use **search criteria** to find records, using logical operators if there is more than one part to the criteria (just like conditions in programming). Here are two examples of search criteria:

- To find the details for a specific candidate:

  CandidateNumber="0010"

- To find students in tutor group SJR who live in Hamsphire:

  County="Hampshire" AND TutorGroup="SJR"

These are Boolean expressions, just like you use in programming

In a relational database there is a built-in feature to select the data you want, these are called **queries**. Queries are used to **interrogate** the database. For example, with a student database you may need to find a specific student's contact details or get a list of all the students in a particular class. A relational database will allow you to construct queries that find data matching specified criteria.

In Microsoft Access the Query By Example (QBE) grid makes it easy to find records that match criteria (example below) but we also need to be able to query a database from our programs. We do this with a purpose-built language called SQL (Structured Query Language). SQL is not specific to MS Access or any other database product; it is an industry standard way of creating and interrogating any relational database. SQL is discussed in detail in the next section.

Here is an example of a query in MS Access to find all students that live in Hampshire:

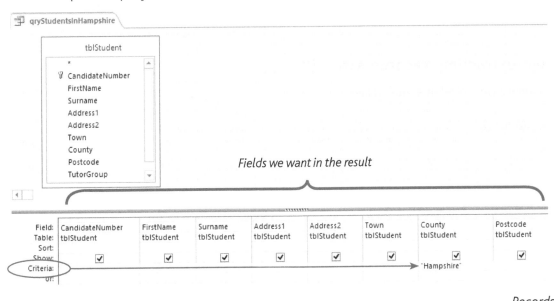

The resulting list:

Records where County = "Hampshire" are selected

Indexing a database to speed up searching

In a small database the query will select all the relevant records very quickly but in a database with thousands or even millions of records it will take longer. One way of speeding up a search would be to sort the records so they are in order. For example, if we sorted all our student records by surname, when we search for students where surname = "Smith", we would find the records quicker. The search algorithm wouldn't need to look at every single record if we know they are already in order.

But then what happens when a Tutor wants to search for students based on the Tutor Group, or the Administration department wants to search based on Postcode? If there were many thousands of records, sorting them every time would be slow and inefficient. Instead of sorting the records, selected fields such as Surname and Postcode can be **indexed**. An index is essentially a list of the order the records would be in if they were sorted on that field. Think of it like an index in a book, where you look up the key word and the index tells you the page number; when you use a database, the software looks up, say, "Smith" in the Surname index and the index tells it the record number to go to.

The primary key field is automatically indexed in a database and is called the primary index. When you create a table, you can specify which other fields are to be indexed, for example any that are commonly used to search on, to speed up searches. An indexed field does not have to be unique.

Query Methods – Using SQL

The AQA Specification says that you should be able to:

- be able to create simple SQL statements to extract, add and edit data stored in databases

Selecting (extracting) records with SQL

Here is the query we looked at earlier, taken from MS Access:

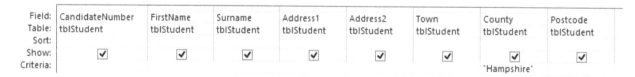

Field:	CandidateNumber	FirstName	Surname	Address1	Address2	Town	County	Postcode
Table:	tblStudent	tblStudent	tblStudent	tblStudent	tblStudent	tblStudent	tblStudent	tblStudent
Sort:								
Show:	✔	✔	✔	✔	✔	✔	✔	✔
Criteria:							"Hampshire"	

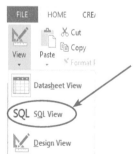

You can look at any Access query in **SQL view** to see how this would be coded (but be aware that Access sometimes puts in more brackets than you really need).

SELECT tblStudent.CandidateNumber, tblStudent.FirstName, tblStudent.Surname, tblStudent.Address1, tblStudent.Address2, tblStudent.Town, tblStudent.County, tblStudent.Postcode

FROM tblStudent

WHERE tblStudent.County="Hampshire";

A query that selects data from one or more tables has this basic syntax (format):

SELECT...   list the field(s) you want displayed here

FROM...   list the table or tables the data will come from here

WHERE...   list search criteria here

ORDER BY...   list field(s) you want the results sorted by here

The SQL coded query will return a result that includes the fields listed in the SELECT part of the statement but you can refer to other fields in the WHERE criteria or ORDER BY part as long as they are fields in the tables listed. An SQL statement always ends with a semicolon. Based on the Student database, the SQL SELECT statement below will list the names and addresses of all the students who live in Basingstoke:

SELECT FirstName, Surname, Address1, Town, County, Postcode

FROM tblStudent

WHERE tblStudent.Town="Basingstoke"

ORDER BY Surname **ASC**;

ORDER BY defaults to ASCending order so you don't have to write "ASC" at the end. If you want descending order you have to add "DESC"

Here are some more examples, based on the Student database:

1   **SELECT** FirstName, Surname, Town

    FROM tblStudent

    WHERE TutorGroup="SJR"

    ORDER BY Surname DESC;

This code will return a list of students, showing just these three fields

This time we are listing the result in descending order so we've added DESC

First Name	Surname	Town
Fred	Smith	Basingstoke
Sally	Jones	Basingstoke
George	Dotts	Reading

This query lists all Mrs Robson's Tutees and where they come from.

2   Perhaps we didn't know the tutor initials were SJR, but wanted details for Mrs Robson's group. We would need to use both tables in the query:

    SELECT FirstName, Surname, Town

    FROM tblTutorGroup, tblStudent

    WHERE tblTutorGroup.TutorName="Mrs Robson"

    AND tblStudent.TutorGroup=tblTutorGroup.TutorGroup;

Notice that we are getting data from two tables now

Because TutorGroup appears in both tables, SQL must reference the field unambiguously by putting the table name in front of the field name.

AND is the logical operator in this condition

Because two tables are involved, the WHERE part is needed to make the connection between the two tables

3 Sometimes we want to match part of a field. For example, all postcodes that start with RG23. To do this we use a wildcard and look for records `like RG23*`

SELECT FirstName, Surname, Postcode

FROM tblStudent

WHERE Postcode like "RG23*";

The * is a wildcard. A wildcard represents anything so in this case we're looking for all students whose postcode starts with RG23 but finishes with anything.

Note:

SQL is generally laid out so it is easy to read, with keywords at the start of a line but SQL is not case-sensitive and it doesn't matter where the line breaks are.

Logical operators in SQL criteria

In the second SQL example, notice that the WHERE criterion consists of two parts with AND in between. This is just like conditions in programming where you can build Boolean expressions with logical operators (AND, OR, NOT). Just like BIDMAS in mathematical calculations, there is also an order of precedence for logical operators. AND takes precedence over OR so you may need extra brackets if the OR parts need resolving first:

  (County="Hampshire") AND (TutorGroup="SJR") OR (TutorGroup="JLH")

The criteria above will return students from tutor group SJR who also live in Hampshire, and all the students in tutor group JLH.

  (County="Hampshire") AND ((TutorGroup="SJR") OR (TutorGroup="JLH"))

This version, with the OR parts bracketed, will return students who are in either of these tutor groups who also live in Hampshire.

Inserting records with SQL

As well as searching for records that meet criteria with the SELECT command, you can use SQL to add records to a database file. The syntax for adding/inserting a record is:

INSERT INTO TableName(FieldName, FieldName, FieldName)

VALUES (Value,Value,Value);

For example, to add a new student to our database:

INSERT INTO tblStudent(CandidateNumber,FirstName,Surname,Address1,Postcode,TutorGroup)

VALUES("0015","Jessica","Smith","37 The Lane","RG22 6GF","SJR");

CandidateNumber	FirstName	Surname	Address1	Address2	Town	County	Postcode	TutorGroup
0015	Jessica	Smith	37 The Lane				RG22 6GF	SJR

Notice that when you insert a record you do not have to fill in every field. You must however fill in the primary key field or it will not insert the record. However, if you are adding a record and filling in all the fields, you do not have to list all the fields in the first part.

INSERT INTO TutorGroup   **VALUES** ("XYZ","Xavier Yeltz", "Block", "987");

Don't need to list field names here if …   *…all four fields have been assigned a value here.*

Updating records with SQL

You can also update existing records with SQL. The syntax for updating a record is:

UPDATE TableName

SET FieldName = value

WHERE criteria; ◄———— *If there is no criteria row then it will replace this field in all the records in that table.*

For example, to change Jessica Smiths Tutor Group in our database:

UPDATE tblStudent

SET TutorGroup = "PLT"

WHERE CandidateNumber="0015";

Deleting records with SQL

You can delete records from a table with SQL. The syntax for deleting a record is:

DELETE FieldName, FieldName, FieldName   (or   *   for all fields/whole record)

FROM TableName

WHERE FieldName=Value;

For example, to delete Candidate Number 0015 from our database:

DELETE *

FROM tblStudent

WHERE CandidateNumber="0015";

Or, to delete Candidate Number 0004's Postcode from our database:

DELETE Postcode

FROM tblStudent

WHERE CandidateNumber="0004";

Deleting a table with SQL

You can delete a whole table using SQL. The syntax for deleting a table is:

DROP TABLE TableName;

For example, to delete the TutorGroup table from our database:

DROP TABLE tblTutorGroup;

Using SQL in program code

> ### The AQA Specification says that you should be able to:
> - have experience of using these SQL statements from within their own coded systems

If you are working with a package like MS Access, then you would probably use the QBE grids to create queries, and possibly attach them to buttons on forms.

If you are just using the relational database as a data structure and are writing a front-end to this in a high level programming language, you will want to manipulate the database using SQL within your program code.

You will need to know how to do this with your own language, possibly for use in the controlled assessments. Typically though you will build up the SQL statement in a string variable and then execute it within the code in some way. The SQL code always uses the same syntax; it is a common standard that allows programmers to access and manipulate relational databases from any language. Here are some examples from Delphi:

    DoCmd.RunSQL "DELETE * FROM Customer WHERE Town='Fleet';"

    DoCmd.RunSQL "INSERT INTO Cars VALUES ('RE09 EFD','Ford','Mondeo','Black');"

    DoCmd.RunSQL "UPDATE Customer SET Contact = 'Fred' WHERE Town='Fleet';"

Often the SQL query will use values from text boxes on a form. For example, if your program has a search feature that the user can type a value into, the program will need to build this value into the search criteria part of the SQL string. The SQL statement is built up as a string, including the quote marks that have to go around the value in the SQL statement. This string is assigned to the variable SQLString.

    SQLString:= "SELECT BookTitle, Publisher, ISBN FROM Books WHERE AuthorName = '";

    SQLString:= SQLString + AuthorName.text +"'ORDER BY Publisher;";

If the text box called AuthorName contained "Susan Robson", the resulting value of SQLString would be:

    "SELECT BookTitle, Publisher, ISBN FROM Books

    WHERE AuthorName = 'Susan Robson' ORDER BY Publisher;"

Once the SQL statement is built, the DoCmd.RunSQL command just references the variable SQLString:

    DoCmd.RunSQL SQLString;

Using Databases from Web-Based Applications

The AQA Specification says that you should be able to:

- be able to use databases from within their own web based applications

To create a database-driven web page you will most likely use a language such as PHP or ASP with HTML and SQL. This book does not aim to teach HTML or any scripting languages but looks at the basic principles. For the controlled assessment tasks you should be able to code basic dynamic web pages in your chosen language, connecting to your chosen database product.

In *Chapter 5: Networking* we looked at the basics of creating a static page in HTML, adding tables to arrange data on the page and using client-side scripting to do some validation on a form. In this chapter we will use the same table tags to present data but the table will be populated from a database.

Populating a web page from a database

Dynamic web pages can be updated from a database. When your browser requests a page from the web server, the web server will fill in the dynamic parts at the server side and then send an up-to-date page to your computer (the client). Hence database driven web-page programming is known as server-side programming.

The page structure will be coded in HTML and HTML tags may also be used in the code to organise the dynamic data in a table structure. As the HTML table tags are embedded in the scripting code, they will be formatted a little differently but essentially the same tags are used to create the table structure. Instead of putting text in the cells, the scripting language reads a row from the response to an SQL query, and displays a field in each cell. In PHP it would look like this:

Static data: Actual data values are coded inside HTML table tags:

```
<tr>
  <td> 1 </td>
  <td> Small box </td>
  <td> 3.10 </td>
</tr>
```

| 1 | Small box | 3.10 |

Dynamic data: The fields are put inside HTML table tags, which are embedded in the PHP code:

```
echo "<tr>";
  echo "<td> {$row["ProdID"]} </td>";
  echo "<td> {$row["Descrip"]} </td>";
  echo "<td> {$row["Price"]} </td>
echo "</tr>";
```

The scripting language will use programming constructs like those discussed in *Chapter 7: Programming Concepts and Algorithms*. As the number of products being displayed on a page may change, the code executed at the server-side will involve a loop that creates table rows for each product until it gets to the end of the list of products from the file or database. In PHP this might look like:

```
while ($row = mysql_fetch_assoc($result )) {

   //code to display each row goes here

}
```

In PHP, curly brackets are used to begin and end sections of code within the loop. The condition in the while loop above just means, "while a row of data exists, put it in a variable called $row". $row is a record variable made up of fields that can be accessed individually:

```
$row["ProdID"]

$row["Descrip"]  etc
```

The web page is created using HTML with (in this case) PHP code within it. The following tags show where the PHP code starts and ends:

```
<?php

// code goes here

?>
```

Within the PHP code you can also embed HTML tags, such as those used to put the fields in the table structure, using the `echo` command (see previous page).

Here is a simple web page in PHP, which gets a list of products from a database table called "Products" using an SQL query. It displays them in a table format using HTML table tags (see code on next page).

File   Edit   View   Favorites   Tools   Help

Product List

Product ID	Description	Price £
1	Small box	3.10
2	Medium box	4.50
3	Large box	8.45
4	Small lid	1.25
5	Medium lid	2.50
6	Large lid	2.99

```
<body>
  <h1>Product List</h1>

  <?php

    // Connect to database
    $dblink = mysql_connect ( "localhost", "Susan", "password" );

    // Run query
    $result = mysql_query("SELECT * FROM BookDB.Products ORDER BY prodID;");

    echo "<table border='1'>";
    // Write table headings
        echo "<tr>";
        echo "<th> ProdID </th>";
        echo "<th> Description </th>";
        echo "<th> Price £ </th>";
        echo "</tr>";

    // Populate table with rows from
    // the result of the query
    while ($row = mysql_fetch_assoc($result )) {
        echo "<tr>";
        echo "<td> {$row["ProdID"]} </td>";
        echo "<td> {$row["Descrip"]} </td>";
        echo "<td> {$row["Price"]} </td>";
        echo "</tr>";
    } //end of while
    echo "</table>"; //end of table

  ?>  //end of php code

</body>
```

This line creates a link to the web server (called "localhost" on my PC), which is where I've hosted my database.

This line runs the SQL query to get all the records from the Products table - the SQL should look familiar.

"echo" is the PHP command to write to the page. These lines create the table heading row

This while loop processes each row in the query result

For each row in the query result, these lines put the separate fields in the table boxes using <td> tags

// This is a comment in PHP

Glossary of Terms

Basic Model

Database/ Flat-File Database	A store of data where data is stored in a single file organised into fields and records.
Relational Database	A store of data organised into related tables of records.
Data Duplication/ Data Redundancy	Where the same data is stored more than once, unnecessarily.
Data Inconsistency	Where different versions of data have different values because duplicate versions have been stored and updated differently.
Entity	A category of, for example, person (e.g. student, customer), object (e.g. classroom, stock item) or event (e.g. holiday booking, TV program) about which data is stored in a database, and which corresponds to a table in the relational database.
Table	A collection of data organised into records and fields within a relational database. A table represents a real-world entity e.g. student, product, employee
Record	Data stored about one instance of an entity i.e. one particular person or object.
Field	One specific data item being stored such as surname or shoe size.
Primary Key	A field in a table that uniquely identifies a record.
Foreign Key	A field in one table, which is the primary key in another table and is used to create a relationship between those two tables.
Relationship	The logical connection between two tables using a primary and foreign key pair.
Query	A feature of a database system that allows the database to be interrogated. It selects records from the database based on specified criteria. In coded systems this is done with SQL.
SQL	Structured Query Language: a high level programming language that is the standard way of searching and manipulating a relational database.
Index	A mechanism for finding records in a file/database more quickly. It stores the logical order that records would have been in, if they had been sorted by a particular field.
Primary Index	The primary key field is always the primary index.
Logical Operator	NOT, AND, OR. Used in complex criteria in queries.

Sample Questions

These questions are similar to the ones you may see in the exam. Good answers to these, along with exam hints and tips, can be found at the end of the book.

1 The two tables Pet and Owner form a relational database used by a vet.

PET

PetID	Name	Animal	OwnerID
15	Barney	Cat	3
23	Spot	Dog	2
33	Jasper	Dog	5
37	Snowflake	Rabbit	6
42	Desmond	Dog	2
45	Indy	Cat	3

OWNER

OwnerID	FirstName	Surname	PhoneNumber
2	Jessica	Mason	01234 829376
3	George	Smith	01234 776255
5	Dev	Patel	01278 987654
6	Sheila	Jameson	01245 636363

(a) State the primary key of the **Owner** table and justify your choice.   [2]

(b) List the results of executing the following SQL query on the database above.

SELECT Pet.Name, Owner.FirstName, Owner.Surname

FROM Owner,Pet

WHERE Animal = "Dog"

AND Owner.OwnerID = Pet.OwnerID   [3]

(c) Write an SQL statement to add the following data to the Pet table.

49	Ginger	Cat	6

      [3]

(d) Describe the role of the **OwnerID** field in the **Pet** table   [3]

2 Describe the difference between a flat file and a relational database, using as an example how data would be stored about customer details and products that they have bought. Explain why a relational database is better than a flat file to store this data.

In this question you will be marked on your ability to use good English, to organise information clearly and to use specialist vocabulary where appropriate. [6]

3 Here is a list of terms connected with databases:

     Primary Key   Record   Index   Field   Foreign Key   Relationship

Complete the table below by adding the correct term for each description:

Database Term	Description
(a)	Can store all the data about a specific person
(b)	Must be a primary key in another table
(c)	Uniquely identifies a record
(d)	Used to speed up searches for specific records

[4]

Chapter 7: Programming Concepts

This topic is all about general programming concepts. As part of GCSE Computer Science you will learn a high level programming language such as Delphi, Python, Java or Visual Basic. This book is not intended to teach you how to program in any particular language but focuses on the key constructs and concepts.

For the purpose of clarity in exam questions AQA have defined a structured way of writing **pseudocode** (a way of outlining the steps of a program, not as detailed as actual code and not in any specific language). This is available on the AQA web page for GCSE Computer Science. This book will use that form of pseudocode to demonstrate the basic concepts but occasionally uses some real code just to illustrate the concept.

Your First Program – Output to User

The first program you write will probably just output "Hello World" – almost a programming tradition. Being able to output messages/information to the user is an important part of any program and a good place to start. In pseudocode an output command will look something like this:

```
OUTPUT "Hello World"
```

In high level programming languages the output commands are usually called output, print or write.

For example:

```
Delphi:      write 'Hello World';
Java:        system.out.println("Hello World");
Python:      print 'Hello World'
```

Input and Identifiers

Just outputting text to the user is going to make a very dull program. At some point the user needs to interact with the program by giving it some data or telling it what to do next, such as picking a menu option. Inputs to the program are data and they must be stored somewhere so the program can use them. When a program is running, it is in the computer's main memory (RAM) so this is where the data needs to be as well. From the computer's point of view, main memory is a series of numbered locations, but people work better with names, so each location that the data occupies is given a unique name called an **identifier**. The data stored in these locations are called **variables** and are referred to by the appropriate identifier.

Variables and Data Types

The AQA specification says that students should:

- understand the different data types available to them. As a minimum, students should know about integer, Boolean, real, character and string data types and how these are represented in the programming language(s) they are using

- be able to explain the purpose of data types within code

Any data that a program uses must be stored in memory locations, each given its own unique identifier, while the program is running. As the program runs, the values in these locations might change, which is why they are called variables. For example: a variable called "total" might change several times as numbers are added to it, or a variable called "surname" will change as the program processes a list of customer orders.

Each variable has a **data type** that defines:

- the type of data that will be stored at the memory location and therefore the operations that can be performed on this data item (you can multiply two numbers but you can't multiply two words)

- how much space will be needed to store that data item

In some programming languages variables are declared at the start of a program so when the program runs, the appropriate amount of memory can be reserved to store the data. The following are examples from a Delphi program (left) and Visual Basic (right):

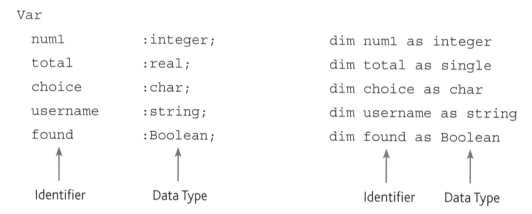

```
Var
    num1         :integer;          dim num1 as integer
    total        :real;            dim total as single
    choice       :char;            dim choice as char
    username     :string;          dim username as string
    found        :Boolean;          dim found as Boolean
```

Identifier   Data Type   Identifier   Data Type

In any high level language in which variables are declared, there is always an identifier part and a data type.

Some languages, for example Python, will assume the data type of a variable based on what is put in it. So 23 will be an integer (whole number) whereas "Fred" will be a string (text). Even if you do not have to declare variables in your particular programming language, it is really important that you understand the different data types and how to work with them in your controlled assessments.

The table below shows some data types and the typical amount of memory that each would need. The programming language that you are using may have different names for some of these; for example, "real" is called "float" in some languages. Your language may also have some additional data types not listed below. The amount of memory used for each data type varies for different programming languages – for example, an integer may need 2 bytes in one language but 4 bytes in another.

Data Type	Type of Data	Typical Amount of Memory
Integer	A whole number, such as 3, 45, -453	2 or 4 bytes
Real/Float	A number with a fractional part such as 34.456, -9.234	4 or 8 bytes
Char/ Character	A single character, where a character can be any letter, digit, punctuation mark or symbol that can be typed.	1 byte
String	Zero or more characters. A string can be null (empty), just one character or several characters. Some programming languages have a default number of characters if the programmer does not specify the maximum size.	1 byte per character in the string
Boolean	A Boolean variable has the value True or False	1 byte

Assignment

Putting an actual value into a variable is called **assignment**. In AQA pseudocode this is shown with a backwards arrow: ←

The diagram below shows some pseudocode that adds two numbers together. This uses three variables, Num1, Num2 and Total.

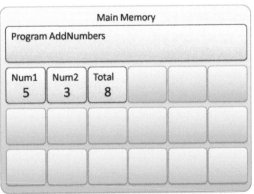

```
NUM1 ← 5
NUM2 ← 3
Total ← Num1 + Num2
OUTPUT Total
```

The previous program will only ever add 5 and 3 together. The following pseudocode shows one way of getting input from the user:

```
Num1 ← USERINPUT

Num2 ← USERINPUT

Total ← Num1+Num2

OUTPUT Total
```

> **! Note:**
>
> If you read the backwards arrow as, "becomes equal to" it will make more sense!

In different languages you will see different ways of coding this. Obviously in your code you can't easily type a backwards arrow, so some languages just use an equals sign:

```
Num1 = 23
```

This means "Num1 becomes equal to 23" or, more technically, that we are assigning the value 23 to the variable called "Num1". This can be confusing as Num1=23 may also be used as a condition when comparing Num1 with the value 23, as in "is Num1 equal to 23?". Some languages, such as VB, just use = and the meaning is clear from the context in which it is used. Some languages have gone for a non-ambiguous version, for example:

Delphi:	`Num1:=23`	for assignment
	`Num1=23`	for comparisons (Boolean expression)
Java and Python:	`Num1=23`	for assignment
	`Num1==23`	for comparisons

Some languages allow you to set several variables to a certain value in one statement/command:

```
Num1, Num2, Total = 0
```

This is really useful at the start of a program where you want to set starting values for variables. This is called **initialisation**. It is important to initialise variables because there may already be values in those memory locations from a previous program or a previous run of this program. Some languages will automatically set numerical variables to zero when you declare them but it is good practice to initialise them anyway, just to be sure.

Constants

The AQA specification says that students should:

- be able to describe the difference between a constant and a variable

- understand when to use constants and variables in problem-solving scenarios

In a program there are certain values that remain the same (constant) while the program runs. For example, the conversion rate between inches and centimetres is always 2.53. The programmer could use the actual number in the code each time but it is considered good practice to give the number a unique name (an **identifier**) and then use that name throughout the program.　**Constants** are usually declared at the start of a program and then referred to as needed in the code.　For example:

At the start of the program:　　CONST **InchToCm** = 2.53

Later in the program code:　　HeightMetric ← HeightInches * **InchToCm**

Note though, that this does not mean that the constant's value will never change during the lifetime of the program. For example, the VAT rate will stay the same (constant) while the program runs in the shop each day but, after the next budget, it may change.　The value allocated to that constant will then need to be edited in the program.

At the start of the program:　　CONST **VATRate** = 0.2

Later in the program code:　　SellPrice ← NetPrice * **VATRate** + NetPrice

The two main benefits of declaring a constant are:

- When its value changes, you only have to edit it in one place rather than looking for every place in the program where you used that number.

- The code will be easier to read and understand because the constant's identifier will be used instead of a number. This makes your code easier to debug and, later on, maintain.

Arrays

The AQA specification says that students should:

- understand and be able to program with 1 and 2 dimensional arrays

Earlier in this chapter we talked about variables.　If we were processing one or two specific data items, then we would have a variable for each of these.　For example, a program that adds two numbers together might use variables called num1, num2 and total, all of type integer.

Often a program will process a number of data items of the same type; for example, a program processing the results of a marathon for 5,000 people who have run a marathon race, may need to sort and print these in order of their race times. All the records need to be held in memory while the sorting is done.

We could use variables called ID1, Result1, ID2, Result2, ID3, Result3... ID5000, Result5000 to store the IDs and times of each runner but most programming languages allow you to use an array to make processing groups of data easier to code.

1-dimensional arrays

An array is a group of data items of the **same data type**, which is stored under one identifier (name) in contiguous (one after another) memory locations. The diagram shows an array called "numbers" with five data items, all of type integer

	1	2	3	4	5
Numbers					

The individual boxes in the array can be used just like variables:

Assign values to them: `Numbers[4]← 27;`

Read values into them from the keyboard or a file: `Numbers[4] ← USERINPUT`

Write the value stored in a box to the screen or a file: `OUTPUT "4th is ", Numbers[4]`

The array below stores 10 test scores for a student using a simple array called **TestScores**. Imagine a table with 1 row of 10 boxes

1	2	3	4	5	6	7	8	9	10

Each box has a numerical reference called a **subscript** or **index**, which is used to refer to that individual data item. For example, the third box in this array is referred to as:

        `TestScores[3]`

At the start of a program the array is defined, in a similar manner to a variable. In Delphi the array declaration for the array shown above would look like this, assuming test scores are whole numbers:

Note:

Some languages start numbering arrays at zero rather than from 1.

        `TestScores : array[1..10] of integer;`

The pseudocode below initialises the array so that each cell contains zero. Just as with variables, it is good practice to initialise arrays so you know that the values in each cell are what you expect at the start of the program:

        `TestScores ← [0,0,0,0,0,0,0,0,0,0]`

The pseudocode algorithm below gets 10 test scores from the user, adds them up and outputs the total:

```
total ← 0

FOR count ← 1 to 5 do
    OUTPUT "Enter Test score ",count,": "
    TestScores[count] ← USERINPUT
    total ← total + TestScores[count]
ENDFOR
OUTPUT "Total is ",total
```

Initialise the variable 'total' to zero at the start

Reads each number into the numbered location in the array, based on the value of 'count' each time. count =1 the first time, 2 the second time etc.

Refers to the current value of count to add a specific number to the total

Note:

If your language does not have a FOR loop you can use a REPEAT or WHILE loops instead, just set your "count" variable to 1 before the loop starts and remember to add one to it inside the loop!

The benefits of using arrays are:

- code is easier to follow and therefore easier to debug and maintain
- a group of data can be easily processed using a loop

(FOR loops are ideal if the language has one)

2-dimensional arrays

In the example above 10 numbers were stored in a 1-dimensional array. These were the test scores for just one student. If you want the program to store test scores for a class of 30 students, you will need more rows. You could use a 2-dimensional array, which would be declared like this in Delphi:

```
ClassScores : array[1..10,1..30] of integer;
```

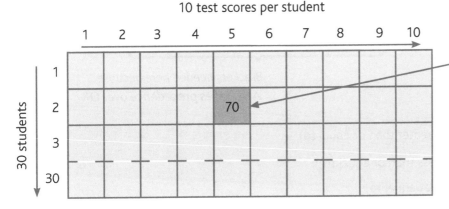

This cell is referred to as:
`ClassScores[5,2]`

If student 2 achieves a test score of 70 in test 5, the assignment in pseudocode looks like this:

`ClassScores[5,2] ← 70`

Boolean Expressions

> ## The AQA specification says that students should:
>
> - use NOT, AND and OR when creating Boolean expressions and have experience in using these operators within coded solutions

When we looked at data types we saw that Boolean variables are either true or false. **Boolean expressions** are also true or false and can be grouped to form more complex Boolean expressions using **logical operators**.

Understanding how Boolean expressions work will also help your programming. In your programs you often use complex Boolean expressions to control loops and selection statements, for example:

```
WHILE (NOT EndOfFile) AND (NOT ItemFound)...
IF (X ≤ 10) OR (CurrentCharNum > LengthOfString) THEN ...
```

You have probably programmed a REPEAT loop to carry on until the user typed an "N" or an "n". The loop would look something like this with the condition at the end:

```
REPEAT
   |
   |
   |
UNTIL (continue = 'N') or (continue = 'n')
```

A Boolean expression

Another Boolean expression

*A condition in programming is made up of **Boolean expressions**, which are either true or false*

Boolean expressions are also used to control selection statements. For example:

```
IF  score > 30 THEN  output "Well done"     ("score>30"  is the condition)
```

Consider an estate agent's program that searches through a file of house details to find properties that match a customer's requirements:

```
IF (NumberOfRooms≥3) AND ((type="House") OR (type="Flat")) THEN  output
```

Brackets needed here because AND takes precedence over OR

! **Note:**

≥	is the same as >=	(greater than or equal to)
≤	is the same as <=	(less than or equal to)
≠	is the same as <> and !=	(not equal to)

Program Data Flow

The AQA specification says that students should:

- understand and be able to describe the basic building blocks of coded solutions (i.e. sequencing, selection and iteration)
- know when to use the different flow control blocks (i.e. sequencing, selection and iteration) to solve a problem

There are three constructs used in programming (in both pseudocode algorithms and in actual code). It is important that you use the most appropriate constructs in your programs to make the code as efficient as possible, as well as making it easier to read, debug and maintain.

Sequence

Sequence is just a matter of writing the steps down in the order they need to happen. For example:

```
price    ←  USERINPUT
quantity ←  USERINPUT
total    ←  quantity * price
OUTPUT "Total price is ", total
```

Selection

There are two basic selection constructs that you will learn when you program. IF...THEN...ELSE allows you to choose between two options. By nesting these or having several in a row you can choose between several options but this is more efficiently achieved by the CASE statement. Both constructs are shown below showing the key words in bold:

```
IF X ≤ 10 THEN
    Z ← Z + 10
ELSE
    Z ← Z - 10
ENDIF
```

Still indent as you would in your programs

Not all programming languages use "ENDIF" but we normally use it in pseudocode algorithms just to be really clear.

The pseudocode over the page shows three different ways of coding selection where there are multiple choices. The example shows a menu system where the user can choose between three options:

Method 1: Using multiple IF statements

```
IF MenuChoice=1 THEN
    Do_this_thing
ENDIF
IF MenuChoice=2 THEN
    Do_the_other_thing
ENDIF
IF MenuChoice=3 THEN
    Self-destruct
ENDIF
```

These are three separate IF...THEN statements so the computer will have to execute the second and third IF statements, even if the user selected '1' from the menu.

This is not efficient coding but it will work.

Method 2: Using multiple nested IF statements

```
IF MenuChoice=1 THEN
    Do_this_thing
ELSE
    IF MenuChoice=2 THEN
        Do_the_other_thing
    ELSE
        IF MenuChoice=3 THEN
            Self-destruct
        ENDIF
    ENDIF
ENDIF
```

This still uses three separate IF...THEN statements but they are nested so that the computer will only execute the IF statement tests until it finds one that is true.

This is more efficient than method 1 but for several choices it is difficult for a programmer to follow.

Method 3: Using a CASE statement:

```
CASE MenuChoice OF
    1: Do_this_thing
    2: Do_the_other_thing
    3: Self-destruct
ELSE
    OUTPUT "You must choose 1 - 3!"
ENDCASE
```

The CASE statement is designed for coding multiple choices in a program, such as a menu of options where the user will enter one choice.

Can you see how much clearer this chunk of code is than the nested IF version above?

Iteration

There are three basic iteration (loop) constructs that you will learn when you program.

The **FOR** loop allows you to execute a group of steps 1 or more times, for a specific number of times.

```
FOR count ← 1 to 10 DO
    OUTPUT count * 3
ENDFOR
```

Sets count to 1 the first time through the loop and then automatically increments it (adds 1)

*Not all programming languages use "**ENDFOR**" but we normally use it in pseudocode just to be really clear.*

A REPEAT loop is controlled by a condition at the end of the loop. It will, therefore, always execute the following steps at least once. Here is an example of an algorithm that uses a REPEAT loop:

```
count ← 1

REPEAT

    OUTPUT count * 3

    count ← count + 1

UNTIL count = 10
```

A **WHILE** loop is controlled by a condition **at the start** of the loop. It will, therefore, execute the following steps **zero or more** times. This is important when you read from a file, for example, when you need to check if the file is empty **before** you try to read from it. Here is an example of an algorithm that uses a WHILE loop:

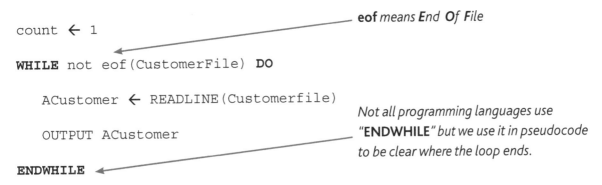

```
count ← 1

WHILE not eof(CustomerFile) DO

    ACustomer ← READLINE(Customerfile)

    OUTPUT ACustomer

ENDWHILE
```

eof means End Of File

*Not all programming languages use "**ENDWHILE**" but we use it in pseudocode to be clear where the loop ends.*

Note:

A **condition** is a **Boolean expression** that will be true or false at a particular point in the program. Conditions are used to control iteration and selection statements.

Algorithms

> **The AQA specification says that students should:**
>
> - understand that algorithms are computational solutions that always finish and return an answer
>
> - be able to interpret simple algorithms to deduce their function
>
> - be able to create algorithms to solve simple problems

When you started programming, your whole program fitted on the screen. It was really easy to see what was going on and fix any problems. As programs get much bigger they become unmanageable so they need to be broken up into smaller sections.

Also, when you start with a user problem in real life, the problem is going to be much more complex than the programs at GCSE. Writing the code is the easy part; working out exactly what the code has to do is more difficult. The series of steps the program has to perform to solve the problem is called an **algorithm**. A working algorithm will always finish and return an answer or perform the task it was supposed to. "Always finishes" is something you may take for granted until you write a program that gets stuck in an infinite loop (always save before you run your program).

Let's take a step back from programming a moment.
Other sorts of algorithm that you may be familiar with are:

- recipes
- directions
- knitting patterns
- instruction for flat-pack furniture

Here's the problem:

How do I get from the Winchester service station on

the M3 to Winchester High Street?

Here is the algorithm: ──────────────────────────►

> Winchester Service Area
> ....
> ....
> Leave the M3 at unction 9, then at roundabout take the 1st exit onto the A272
> **Signposted Winchester, Petersfield, Alton**
> ....
> ....
> At Spitfire Roundabout take the 2nd exit onto the A31
> **Signposted Winchester**
> ....
> ....
> At roundabout take the 1st exit onto Bar End Road – B3404
> **Signposted Winchester**
> ....
> ....
> At traffic signals turn right onto Bar End Road – B3404
> **Signposted City Centre**
> ....
> ....
> At roundabout take the 1st exit onto Bridge Street – B3404
> **Signposted City Centre**
> ....

An algorithm does not have to be written in code. The first steps to working out the design will be to draw diagrams and/or list the steps involved. The next section focuses on how to break down the problem and then structure a solution using some standard tools called structure diagrams and flowcharts. Only when the system has some structure can you start coding it effectively. Pseudocode is the first step to actual code as it outlines the algorithm in programming constructs but doesn't rely on any specific language syntax.

User Requirement → Structure Chart → Flowchart → Pseudocode → Actual Program Code

Program Structure and Algorithm Design

The AQA specification says that students should:

- understand the need for structure when designing coded solutions to problems
- understand how problems can be broken down into smaller problems and how these steps can be represented by the use of devices such as flowcharts and structure diagrams

Being a good programmer is all about being able to break a problem down into smaller parts and construct a solution. We need to break the problem down into sections (modules) so that we can work with it more easily. Structuring a system into manageable modules is important for several reasons:

- Different people can work on different sections at the same time.
- Some parts may be used several times in a system. By making these parts into separate modules, they can be re-used more easily by calling that module, not writing duplicate code.
- Modules of code can be tested on their own before being put together in the whole system; this makes it much easier to find bugs and fix them
- A modular system is much easier to understand and maintain later on.

Structure charts

One tool for breaking a problem/system down into modules small enough to code separately is a **structure diagram**. The type described here is called a Jackson Structure Diagram (an industry-recognised tool). Let's consider a game of "Noughts and Crosses". Two players take it in turns to put their cross or nought in the grid. The program has to check that the user has picked an empty square and then check if they have now got three crosses/noughts in a row.

Here is a high level diagram for "Noughts and Crosses".

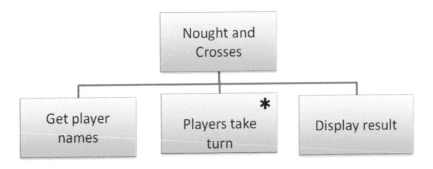

The diagram starts with a box at the top that represents the whole program. The whole program can then be broken down into smaller components: getting the names of the players, playing the actual game in turns and then displaying the result, such as "Jane has won!" The second row of boxes is read left to right and represents a **sequence**. These boxes happen one after another, in that order. (Remember the three programming constructs that we discussed earlier in the chapter: sequence, selection and iteration).

The next step is to break each of these boxes down into more detail.

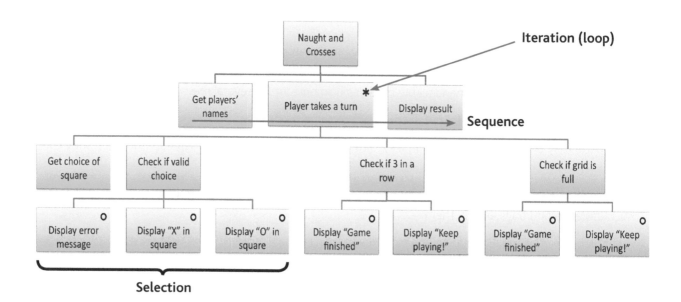

As well as the **sequence** of boxes going left to right in the second layer, the section of the program where a player takes a turn will need to be repeated several times before the game is completed. The star in the corner of the box indicates a box that may happen several times and represents **iteration** or a loop in the program.

The box that says "Check if valid choice" checks that the user has picked an empty square. Checking that the input data is sensible is called **validation**. This section of the program will do one of three things: it will either display a cross in the box chosen or display a nought in the box chosen or, if the selection wasn't valid, it will display an error message. The little circles in the corner of these boxes show that the program will do just one of these; this represents **selection** (think of the circles as "o" for "or"!).

Once the structure chart has refined the program down into small enough sections to code, the programmer can use flowcharts to design the algorithm for that particular module.

Flowcharts

A flowchart is an industry-standard design tool, which is used to show an algorithm diagrammatically. There are standard symbols that you will need to understand:

Terminators: just show where the algorithm starts and finishes!

Input/Output box: Shows an input to the system or output from it. Can be something that the user types in or scans, such as a ProductID on a barcode.

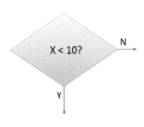

Decision box: always asks a question and has different routes out depending on the answer. In this case if the number "X" is less than 10 you go down, if it isn't you go right.

Process: something that happens, always includes a verb! For example, "add 10 to X" or "store surname to customer database"

Storage: could be a file or database

This very simple example shows the algorithm for taking a pizza order. The program must get the pizza size first and then get one or more toppings.

Notice the following:

- There is a loop to get more than one topping. This loop is controlled by the decision box that asks, "Enough toppings?" If the answer is "Yes" then the program stops, otherwise it keeps asking for the next topping.

- The line that loops around joins the middle of a line, it does not come into a box.

Here is a more complex system requirement. The problem is as follows:

- A computerised form prompts a user to enter their email address.

- A validation rule checks if the address has an @ symbol in it. If it doesn't, an error message is displayed, the text box is cleared and the system asks the user to enter the email address again. This continues until an appropriate address is entered.

- The system then checks that the email address has been typed in lowercase, if not it converts it to lowercase.

- Once the email address is ok it is stored in the customer database.

The flowchart for this could be as follows:

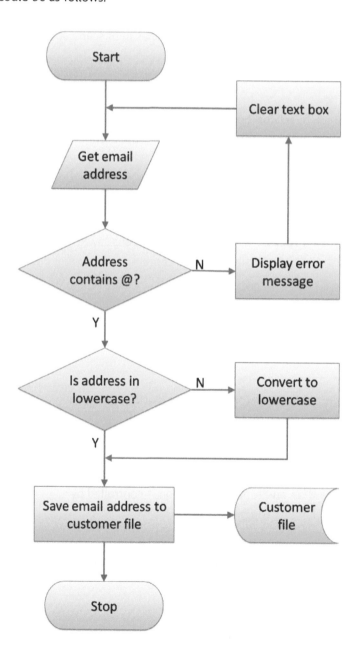

Pseudocode

Pseudocode is used to write an algorithm in programming-style constructs but not in an actual programming language. You do not need to worry about the detailed syntax or be precise about how the code will do something; you just describe the steps you will need in your program. As we said before, an algorithm is a series of steps to solve a problem so that is all you are doing at this stage.

Once you have fairly detailed pseudocode you can use it as comments in your program and write the actual code under each step!

If we convert the flowchart from the previous section into pseudocode it would look something like this:

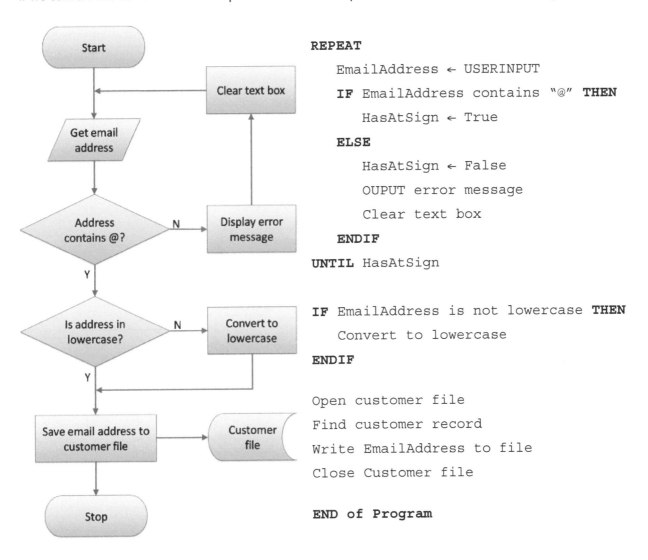

```
REPEAT
    EmailAddress ← USERINPUT
    IF EmailAddress contains "@" THEN
        HasAtSign ← True
    ELSE
        HasAtSign ← False
        OUPUT error message
        Clear text box
    ENDIF
UNTIL HasAtSign

IF EmailAddress is not lowercase THEN
    Convert to lowercase
ENDIF

Open customer file
Find customer record
Write EmailAddress to file
Close Customer file

END of Program
```

In pseudocode you can use phrases like, `IF EmailAddress contains "@" THEN`… At this stage a general statement is fine. When you write the actual code you will need to use the appropriate string-handling function, for example:

$$IF \ Pos(variable,'@') <> 0 \ THEN…$$

(if the position of @ in the variable is 0 then it hasn't been found in the string)

Notice that the pseudocode is indented like a real program. This is good practice and makes your algorithm easier to follow. Also, get into the habit of naming items without spaces. For example, here we've used "EmailAddress". The **PascalCase** format (all words capitalised but no spaces) makes it easy to read and means you don't need to use spaces or underscores. You cannot use spaces in identifiers in any programming language so don't use them in your design.

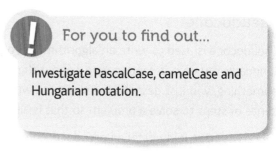

For you to find out...

Investigate PascalCase, camelCase and Hungarian notation.

From structure chart to flowchart

Earlier in the chapter we used a structure chart to break down a game of noughts and crosses into smaller modules. In the structure diagram the player has just entered their choice (greyed out in the diagram below) and then this module validates the data entered:

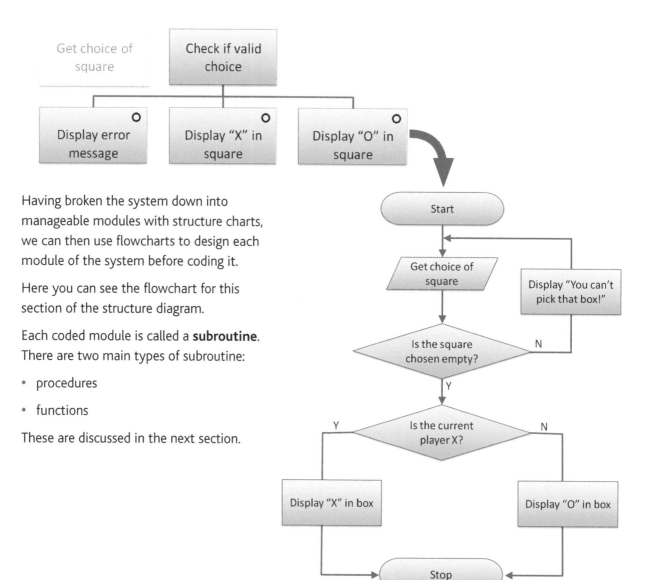

Having broken the system down into manageable modules with structure charts, we can then use flowcharts to design each module of the system before coding it.

Here you can see the flowchart for this section of the structure diagram.

Each coded module is called a **subroutine**. There are two main types of subroutine:

• procedures

• functions

These are discussed in the next section.

Procedures and Functions

The AQA specification says that students should:

- understand what procedures and functions are in programming terms

- know when the use of a procedure or function would make sense and would simplify the coded solution

- know how to write and use their own simple procedures and functions

Procedures

A **procedure** is a self-contained section of code that performs a specific task. It may return one or more values but doesn't have to.

Imagine a recipe for a lemon meringue pie. You could have the recipe written out in one long list of instructions but it might be easier to separate out instructions for making pastry and making meringue, especially as these same instructions will be used in several other recipes as well.

The recipe for Lemon Meringue Pie might say:

1. Make short-crust pastry (see Recipe 5) ←——————

2. Make the meringue (see Recipe 12)

3. Mix the lemon rind, sugar etc

Recipe 5 is a separate recipe (module), which can be referred to whenever a recipe needs pastry

Programs are similar. If you have some code that does a specific task, it can be written as a self-contained procedure. It can then be used from anywhere in the program as needed, without writing all the instructions out again and again.

In a system that has several parts to it, perhaps selected from a menu, it is much easier to write and debug your code if it is written in procedures. The main program might be a CASE statement that calls the procedures to process each menu choice (this is pseudocode but will look similar in your language):

```
CASE choice OF
    1: AddNewCar
    2: FindCarDetails
    3: ListCarsByMake
ENDCASE
```

These are procedure names. Depending on which menu option is chosen, the relevant procedure is called.

You can see from this example that using procedures makes the program structure really clear. Another benefit is that each procedure can be written and tested in isolation from the other modules. This makes debugging much easier and, in the future, the program will be easier to maintain.

Each procedure will be self-contained, a bit like a mini-program within a program. In pseudocode we would write a procedure like this:

```
PROCEDURE FindCarDetails()
    RegNum ← USERINPUT
    Found ← False
    Count ← 1
    WHILE (NOT eof(CarFile)) and (NOT found) DO
        OneCar ← READLINE(CarFile, count)
        IF  OneCar.RegNo = RegNum THEN
            WRITE OneCar
            Found ← True
        ENDIF
        Count ← count + 1
    ENDWHILE
    IF found=False THEN
        WRITE "Not found"
    ENDIF
ENDPROCEDURE
```

Functions

Functions are similar to procedures; they are self-contained sections of code. The key difference is that they always return a single value. You have used functions in a spreadsheet to do things like SUM and COUNT. These always operate on something in brackets and give you a result, a single answer that appears in the cell:

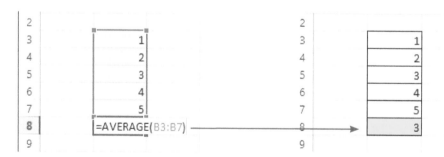

In the spreadsheet above, the function is called AVERAGE. The data it is working on (the range of cells B3 to B7) is in brackets. In programming the principle is the same: you name the function and then put the data it is going to use in brackets. A function always returns a single value so it can also be used in an expression:

```
Hypotenuse ← SquareRoot(SideOne*SideOne+SideTwo*SideTwo)

postcode ← uppercase(postcode)
```

Notice that in the second example the value returned is a string; it doesn't have to be a number.

Here is a sample function written in pseudocode to convert centimetres to inches:

```
FUNCTION cmsToInches(cm)
    inches ← cm / 2.53
    RETURN inches
ENDFUNCTION
```

Notice the statement here says RETURN. A function must return a single value!

It could be used in a line of code like this:

```
height ← USERINPUT
WRITE "Your height in inches is", cmsToInches(height)
```

Parameter passing in functions and procedures

The AQA specification says that students should:

- understand what a parameter is when working with procedures and functions
- know how to use parameters when creating efficient solutions to problems
- understand the concepts of parameters and return values when working with procedures and functions

Converting centimetres to inches is a function that could be used on lots of variables in a program, for example a program that designs furniture might process the height, width and depth of a piece of furniture. If the program has variables called "height", "width" and "depth" you have to have a way of calling the "cmsToInches" function and telling it to use these different variables. This is called parameter passing.

This function can be called as follows:

```
cmsToInches (height);
cmsToInches (width);
cmsToInches (depth);
cmsToInches (23.5);
```

You can call a procedure and pass it the value of a variable or an actual value. This is known as the actual parameter.

Looking at the function at the top of the page again, you can see that the function uses a variable called "cm". When the function is called, the value of the variable in the brackets (height or width or depth) is put into the variable "cm". This is passing the parameter. This means that the function can be called from different places in the main program and pass different data into the function but only needs to be coded once.

```
FUNCTION cmsToInches(cm)
    inches ← cm / 2.53
    RETURN inches
ENDFUNCTION
```

Notice the function heading now has a variable name in the brackets, known as the formal parameter.

"cm" is the variable used in the function even if the function was called with "height".

Built-in functions and procedures

The AQA specification says that students should:

- use common built-in functions in their chosen language(s) when coding solutions to problems

- know about and be able to describe common built-in functions in their chosen language(s)

Each language will have its own built-in procedures and functions that you are probably already using. Procedures will perform a task of some sort, such as reading input into the program from the keyboard or writing output to the screen or a file.

In Delphi some examples of built-in procedures are:

```
Writeln('Hello World');        writes the text "Hello World" to the screen

Readln(Num1);                  reads data from the keyboard into the variable called "Num1"
```

In Delphi some examples of built-in functions are:

```
Length('penguins')        returns 8

Pos('Susan Robson',' ')   returns 6, the position of the space in the string "Susan Robson"

LeftStr('Pink Roses',4)   returns "Pink", the leftmost 4 characters of the string
```

You will need to be aware of the functions and procedures available in your language so that you can use them effectively in your controlled assessments.

Scope of Variables, Constants, Functions and Procedures

The AQA specification says that students should:

- know what is meant by the scope of a variable, constant, function or procedure

- be able to identify what value a particular variable will hold at a given point in the code

Variables can be declared in the main part of a program so that they can be accessed anywhere in the code, including within procedures and functions. These are called **global variables**.

However, if you have broken your system down into modules and different people are coding separate parts then using global variables gets difficult to manage. Each person will want their own variables for their bit of code. In this case you would declare variables within a function or procedure. These are called **local variables** and are only available within that subroutine.

When a function or procedure is executed, it will automatically use the variables found locally, even if there is a global variable with the same name. If the variable is not found locally then the procedure will use the global variable. This means that the same variable identifiers can be used in several different procedures. This is useful if different people are writing different sections of the program.

Here is an outline program in pseudocode, with global and local variables:

```
PROGRAM DoSomeStuff

    #Global variables here
    TheAnswer : integer
    Count     : integer

    PROCEDURE ThreeTimesTable()
        #local variables here
        Count : integer
        #Procedure starts here
        Count ← 1
        REPEAT
           OUTPUT Count * 3
           Count ← Count + 1
        UNTIL Count = 5
    ENDPROCEDURE

    #start of main program here
    Count ← 33
    CALL ThreeTimesTable
    TheAnswer ← 10 * Count;
    OUTPUT "The answer is ",TheAnswer

ENDPROGRAM
```

Count is declared locally in the procedure as well as globally

Here the procedure uses the local variable

Here the main program uses the global variable, which will hold a different value from the one declared in the procedure

```
3
6
9
12
15
The answer is 330
```

This is the output screen for this algorithm/program.

The program above is obviously daft but it illustrates the point. It is considered good practice to always declare variables as locally as possible. Variables used to control loops, such as "Count" should always be local to that function or procedure. You only declare variables globally if you need to use this data in more than one procedure.

When a variable is described as being local or global, this is referred to as the **scope** of the variable. The scope defines whether the variable can be changed just within a procedure or anywhere in the whole program.

Types of Error

> ## The AQA specification says that students should:
>
> - be able to discuss and identify the different types of errors that can occur within code (i.e. syntax, run-time and logical)
>
> - understand that some errors will occur during the execution of the code

When you write a program in a high level programming language a translator will scan each line of code and convert it into machine code, which the computer can then execute. As you will already have found out, programming is not as easy as it looks!

- Firstly, it is very easy to make mistakes typing in the code, for example typing "prnt" instead of "print". These are **syntax errors**

- Secondly, once you have corrected all the syntax errors, the code may run but not do what you want. This means there are **logic errors** in your program.

Syntax errors

The translator expects commands to have a certain format, called syntax, just like a sentence in English has grammar rules. Syntax is the set of rules that states how each command should be formatted. For example, in Delphi you would define variables in the format:

```
VariableName : Datatype;
```

The compiler knows that this statement must have an identifier followed by a colon, followed by a recognised data type and a semi-colon at the end. Spaces don't matter.

Without the correct key words the compiler will not be able to translate the program into machine code and it will give a syntax error. A program will not compile and run if there are syntax errors.

> **! Note:**
>
> If you spell identifiers, such as variable names, incorrectly this is not a problem, as long as you always spell them wrong in the same way.

Some common syntax errors include:

- Mistyping a key word: WRIET instead of WRITE

- Missing key words out of constructs such as starting a REPEAT loop but not writing UNTIL anywhere

- Opening brackets but not closing them

- Not having the right number of parameters inside brackets for functions, for example: `Answer=round(TheNumber)` will give a syntax error if the language expects another parameter to state the number of decimal places: `Answer=round(TheNumber,2)`

Logic errors

Once the code is written correctly, with no syntax errors, the program will run. Just because the program will run does not mean that it is working correctly though! Often we run the program and it doesn't do quite what we expected. This is called a **logic error**.

Typical logic errors that you have probably coded already include:

* Missing brackets from mathematical calculations:

```
NetPay ← GrossPay - TaxFreePart * TaxRate
```

Is not the same as:

```
NetPay ← (GrossPay - TaxFreePart) * TaxRate
```

Note:

Remember BIDMAS?
Brackets first, then multiply and divide, then add and subtract.

* Loops that do not execute the correct number of times because a condition states `X>10` instead of `X>=10`.

* Variables that have not been initialised, or have been initialised in the wrong place (often incorrectly initialised inside the loop instead of just before it).

* Flawed algorithms that just don't do what they were intended to do. Capturing all of the complexities of real-life scenarios in code is difficult and users always manage to do something to the input that you didn't cater for!

Often these logic errors are hard to spot. You should always do a visual check of output to check it isn't ridiculous but you also need to do some systematic testing to make sure the program really does behave as expected.

Run-time errors

Run-time errors occur once a program has started running. Sometimes the program will run and sometimes it might crash. This is because there are some things outside of the control of your program, such as the input the user supplies or files that the program will refer to.

Here are some examples of things that may cause run-time errors:

* When a program is expecting user input that is one data type but the input from the user is another. For example: an integer is expected but the user types some text

* When the computer tries to divide by a variable that has the value zero

* When the program tries to open a file that no longer exists

* When the program tries to read from a file that is empty

* When the computer runs out of memory for some reason

Detecting Errors in Code

> ### The AQA specification says that students should:
> - be able to detect and correct errors in simple algorithms

Three types of error have been defined: syntax errors, run-time errors and logic errors. This section looks at how you can detect each error type.

- Once you have structured your program and designed algorithms for each part you could start coding the program. However, before you do that, you should check that your algorithm is doing what you expected. You can use a trace table to do this.

- Having tested the logic, you then write the code. The Integrated Development Environment (IDE) you use will help you find syntax errors. You need to get rid of all of these before the program will run.

- Even if it runs, it may not work as expected (because it still has logic errors in it) or it may crash because of a run-time error. The IDE includes tools that will help you figure out why.

Using trace tables to detect logic errors

> ### The AQA specification says that students should:
> - be able to use trace tables to check their code for errors

Logic errors are hard to find. Before you actually code your solution it is good idea to check the basic logic of your algorithm. You can do this using a trace table. A trace table is a standard tool for tracking how the value of each variable changes as you go through your algorithm line by line.

Here is a basic algorithm to generate a times table:

```
TimesTable ← USERINPUT
FOR Count ← 1 to 6 DO
   OUTPUT count*TimesTable
ENDFOR
```

Assuming a user types in 4 when prompted, a trace table can be used to track the value of each variable as the lines of the algorithm are followed.

Notice that "4" was only written in once. Only write in the value of a variable if it changes.

The current value of a variable is the last one in that column.

TimesTable	Count	Output
4	1	4
	2	8
	3	12
	4	16
	5	20
	6	24

Here is another example of a trace table being used to solve issues with an algorithm:

The algorithm is designed to work out the average of test scores for a class of 10 students. The scores have already been input into an array called "scores". The average should be the sum of the scores divided by the number of scores. Here is the algorithm:

```
Count ← 1
TotalScore ← 0
REPEAT
    TotalScore ← TotalScore + Scores[Count]
    Count ← Count + 1
UNTIL Count = 10
OUTPUT TotalScore/10
```

Let's assume we have the following scores (out of 10) in the array:

Scores:

1	2	3	4	5	6	7	8	9	10
4	6	7	2	5	7	8	9	10	7

The total of these scores is 65

The average should be 65/10 = 6.5

The trace table for this algorithm looks like this:

TotalScore	Count	Output
0	1	
4	2	
10	3	
17	4	
19	5	
24	6	
31	7	
39	8	
48	9	
58	10	5.8

The total of these scores is 58.

This makes the average 5.8 ✕

The trace table shows that we exited the loop because count = 10, without processing the 10th result!

The algorithm needs adjusting so the loop says:

```
Until Count = 11
```

or

```
Until Count > 10
```

Integrated Development Environment IDE

When you create a program you will be using a software package that helps you write the code more easily. This is called an **Integrated Development Environment or IDE**.

The screenshot below shows the form design view in the Delphi XE3 IDE. The key features labeled are common to most IDEs.

An overview of the program files that make up a "project". A project may consist of many different forms, all connected together.

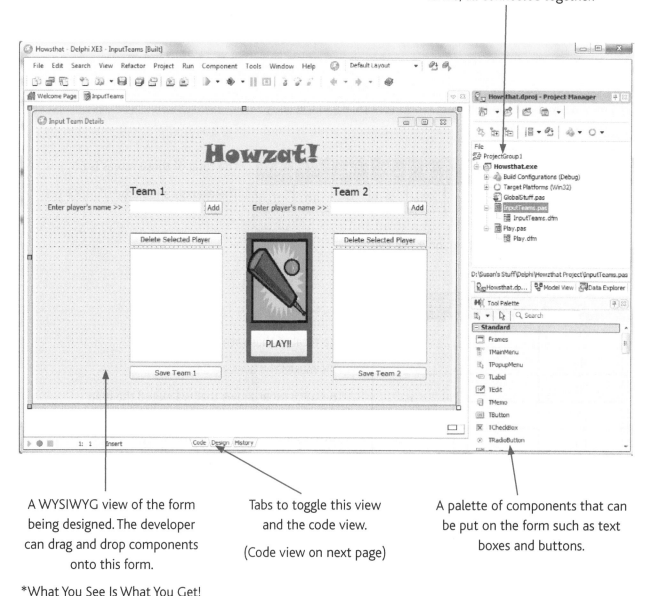

A WYSIWYG view of the form being designed. The developer can drag and drop components onto this form.

*What You See Is What You Get!

Tabs to toggle this view and the code view.

(Code view on next page)

A palette of components that can be put on the form such as text boxes and buttons.

Using IDE Tools to Detect Errors in Code

The AQA specification says that students should:

- know how to detect errors at execution time and how to handle those errors to prevent the program from crashing where desirable

- understand that some errors can be detected and corrected during the coding stage

- understand that computer programs can be developed with tools to help the programmer detect and deal with errors (e.g. Watch, Breakpoint, Step)

Using the editing environment to detect errors

When you write the code the IDE will provide helpful features in the **editing environment** such as colour-coding key words, numbering the lines and even auto completing constructs for you.

The line numbers make it easy to see which bit of code an error message relates to. The auto completion of constructs reduces errors such as missing "ends", or starting a "repeat" loop and forgetting the "until" part.

The editing environment will highlight syntax errors in some way. This IDE will underline errors in red as well as flag line numbers and associated error messages in a separate error window. Beware though, the syntax error isn't always on the highlighted line! If you miss out punctuation or key words that finish a statement or construct, the error may be flagged at the start of the next line because it wasn't expected yet.

Using the run-time environment to detect errors

When you run the program the IDE will provide the translator needed to run the program. The screen and the feedback you see when you try to run the program are provided by the **run-time environment**.

```
procedure TfrmTeamInput.btnT2SaveClick(Sender: TObject);
begin
  reset(team1);
  lstT2Players.ItemIndex:=0;
  while lstT2Players.ItemIndex+1<lstT2Players.Items.Count do
  begin
    with aPlayer do
    begin
      PlayerID:=lstT2Players.ItemIndex+1;
      PlayerName:=lstT2Players.Items.Text;
      NumRuns:=0;
      HowOut:=Not Out;
    end;  // of building one player record
    write(Team2,aPlayer);
    lstT2Players.ItemIndex:=lstT2Players.ItemIndex+1;
  end;  // of adding one player to the file
end;
```

155: 19   Insert   Modified   Code / Design / History

Messages

[dcc32 Error] InputTeams.pas(155): E2003 Undeclared identifier: 'Out'
[dcc32 Fatal Error] Howsthat.dpr(5): F2063 Could not compile used unit 'InputTeams.pas'
Failed

Build | Output

When you try to run the program the IDE will generate error messages in a diagnostics window.

Notice how the IDE has highlighted the line. This is the line causing the error and the message below that says, "Undeclared identifier 'Out'" because the words "Not Out" should be in quote marks in the code.

Compiling the program will highlight syntax errors but once it is running you might still have run-time errors or logic errors to find.

There are other debugging tools that allow the programmer to pause the running program at a certain line and then step through the code a line at a time. This is called a **breakpoint** and is a very useful way of seeing if loops and selection statements are operating as expected. The programmer can also check the values of certain variables at each step.

In some IDEs you can also set up a **watch** on one or more variables. When the program runs, the runtime environment will record and display how the value of those variables changes. This allows the programmer to see how values are assigned to variables at runtime, a bit like doing a manual trace table, and you can also set a breakpoint so that the program pauses if a variable reaches a certain value.

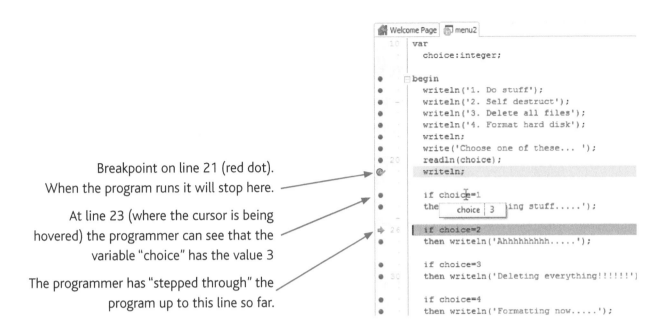

Breakpoint on line 21 (red dot). When the program runs it will stop here.

At line 23 (where the cursor is being hovered) the programmer can see that the variable "choice" has the value 3

The programmer has "stepped through" the program up to this line so far.

In this case there is a breakpoint at line 21 so the programmer can then step through the program one line at a time. The programmer can hover over a variable to see what value it has. Here you can see that "choice" has the value 3. Sometimes the value isn't what you'd expect.

Writing code to handle run-time errors

We have already looked at using the run-time environment to find out where the code fails but sometimes we need to make sure our code takes into account things that might cause our programs to crash.

All of these run-time errors can be avoided by coding **error handling** into our programs. Most languages will have a way of error handling so you need to know how it works in your language. Some examples are:

Python	Try ... Except ...
Delphi	Try ... Except ...
Java	Try ... Catch ...

The "try" part is the instruction that might cause an error. The "except" or "catch" part is what you want to happen if the code fails, instead of your program just crashing. For example, in pseudocode:

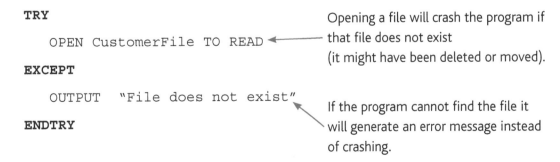

```
TRY
    OPEN CustomerFile TO READ
EXCEPT
    OUTPUT  "File does not exist"
ENDTRY
```

Opening a file will crash the program if that file does not exist
(it might have been deleted or moved).

If the program cannot find the file it will generate an error message instead of crashing.

Data Structures

The AQA specification says that students should:

- be able to explain what a data structure is

- understand and be able to explain why data structures can make coding a solution simpler

- be able to produce their own data types that go beyond the built-in structures of the language(s) they are using, such as arrays or lists. These could include, for example, records in Delphi, structs in C or classes in Python and Java. The actual structures would depend on the language(s) being used by the students

Earlier in the chapter we looked at arrays. An array is a collection of data items stored under one identifier so that the data items can easily be processed. When data items are grouped together so they can be treated as a set of data, this is referred to as a **data structure**.

Records

Most languages will allow you to define arrays quite easily but sometimes you need to define your own data structures. Imagine a program for a car sales showroom. If your program is going to process details about cars, it will be easier to create a record structure to hold all of the car details rather than storing them as one long string of text or lots of separate variables. The data cannot be held in an array because the separate data items about each car are not all of the same data type.

Here is a text file with some car details in it:

```
RE09 HSD, Ford, Focus, 5, 12/10/2009
SW12 SDF, Vauxhall, Corsa, 3, 23/9/2012
BN59 WJR, Nissan, Juke, 4, 1/6/2009
```

We could process this file as lines of text but it would be preferable to define a data structure called a **record**. In Delphi a programmer could define this record type as follows:

```
type TCar = record
        RegNo:string[8];
        Make:string[15];
        Model:string[15];
        NumDoors:integer;
        DateRegistered:date;
    end;
```

Hint: if you put "T" in front of a type name it makes it obvious it is a type and not a variable!

Individual data items within a record are called fields

Having defined a record as a data type, the programmer can create variables having this new data type, for example a variable called `MyCar` of `Type TCar`. The program can then refer to the individual components (fields) of the record. For example, in pseudocode:

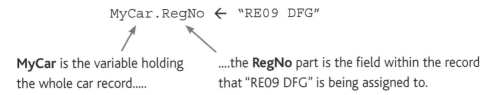

MyCar.RegNo ← "RE09 DFG"

MyCar is the variable holding the whole car record.....

....the **RegNo** part is the field within the record that "RE09 DFG" is being assigned to.

This dot notation is common to many programming languages but check how it works in the one you are using.

Not all languages use the same terminology. For example, in C, you can define a record structure in much the same way as in Delphi but it is called a **struct**. Here is an example in C, where the record stores bank account details:

```
struct account {
    int account_number;
    char first_name[25];
    char last_name[25];
    float balance;
};
```

Keyword is **struct** instead of **record** and curly brackets group the fields.

Individual data items within a record are called fields

Handling External Data

You can get users to input data as required but often we need to process bulk data from a file. In this GCSE you should know how to access data in a text file and a database, using your chosen language. These are skills that will be tested in the controlled assessments, where you will need to know how to use files. The basic principles are outlined below using pseudocode examples to illustrate.

Handling text files

The AQA specification says that students should:

- know how to use an external text file to read and write data in a way that is appropriate for the programming language(s) used and the problem being solved

Text files contain text that is in lines. There is no other structure, unlike files of records. When you read from a text file you can only read a whole line at a time. When you write to it you can only write one line at a time.

Normally you would need to read through a text file one line at a time to get to a specific line but, for writing algorithms in pseudocode, AQA has used this format to read a specific line number from a file or write a line to a file:

variable ← READLINE(Filename,3)

WRITELINE(Filename,3,variable)

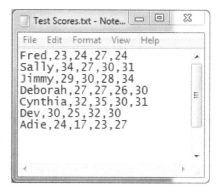

The screenshot to the right shows a simple text file, which could be the output from a program that processes students' test scores. To find a student's score the program would read lines from the file until it found that student's name. This would involve reading the whole line and then finding the name part to compare with the name being searched for.

The algorithm might look like this:

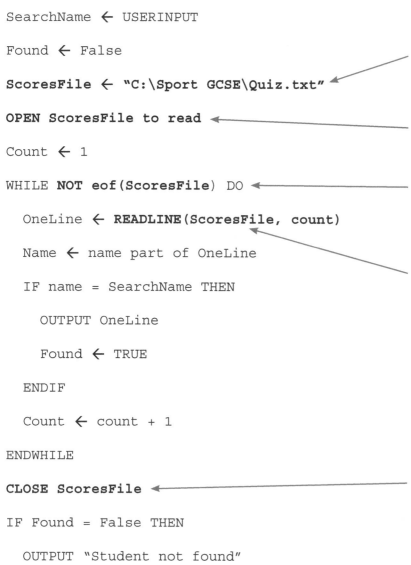

SearchName ← USERINPUT

Found ← False

Tell the program where the file is and allocate it an identifier to use in the program

ScoresFile ← "C:\Sport GCSE\Quiz.txt"

OPEN ScoresFile to read

Open the file in READ mode - this opens an existing file pointing to the first line

Count ← 1

WHILE NOT eof(ScoresFile) DO

eof (End of File) is a standard term used when processing a file

OneLine ← READLINE(ScoresFile, count)

Name ← name part of OneLine

IF name = SearchName THEN

READ a line from the file - you'll need a string variable to put the line of text into. Call it something obvious such as "OneScore" or "OneLine"!

OUTPUT OneLine

Found ← TRUE

ENDIF

Count ← count + 1

ENDWHILE

Remember to close the file as soon as you can in your code - unclosed files will cause runtime errors.

CLOSE ScoresFile

IF Found = False THEN

OUTPUT "Student not found"

ENDIF

In any programming language you will need to follow these steps to access data in the text file:

- Tell the program where the file is

- Open the file to READ from it (opens the file with a pointer pointing to the first line)

- Read a line/lines of text from the file (this will automatically move the pointer down to the next line)

- Close the file

Writing to the file follows the same idea:

- Open the file to WRITE to.

- To add/append to the file the program must be pointing at the end of the file (read lines until End of File, and then write the new one).

- To edit a line, the new line is simply written over the old one.

- And remember to close the file at the end!

Comma-Separated Value files

Text files can contain more complex data and sometimes you will see comma-separated value files that attempt to structure the line of text into fields, a bit like fields in a record of a database. The filename will have the suffix .csv but it is still essentially a text file. You still have lines of text, the only difference is that commas separate each field. Some programs will recognise this format and interpret it as separate data items on a line. Spreadsheets will do this. Here is a csv file with more students' scores in it.

Viewed in notepad, as a text file

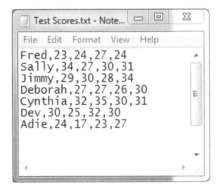

How it looks if you open it in Excel

	A	B	C	D	E
1	Fred	23	24	27	24
2	Sally	34	27	30	31
3	Jimmy	29	30	28	34
4	Deborah	27	27	26	30
5	Cynthia	32	35	30	31
6	Dev	30	25	32	30
7	Adie	24	17	23	27

You can process the csv file in exactly the same way as a text file. Use string handling commands to find the commas and the text between commas. You can use variables to store the separate parts of the line but being able to create a record structure in the program would be useful here (see p126-127 on data structures).

Alternatively, if the data looks like a file of records, perhaps they should be stored in a database instead of a csv file. This might not always be practical though. Often csv files are used to transfer data between systems as it is a very simple format supported by many other programs, databases and spreadsheets.

Handling database files

The AQA specification says that students should:

- know how to read and write data from an external database in a way that is appropriate for the programming language(s) used and the problem being solved

If a program is using data stored in a database then you need to tell the program about the files or tables that it will need to access. How you do this will depend on the language you are using. You will need to know how to do this in your language for the controlled assessments.

Once you have connected your program to the database in some way, the records of data are read from the files or tables and processed in the same way as the records we looked at earlier in the chapter.

Use of External Code Sources

The AQA specification says that students should:

- know of the existence of external code sources
- know how to integrate code from these sources into their own code
- be able to explain the advantages and disadvantages of using such sources

Using library programs

How many different programs have you used where you have to open a file? They all look very similar and all use the same concepts such as browsing through Windows Explorer folder structures to find the file you want. Here is an example of iTunes using the Windows Explorer functionality:

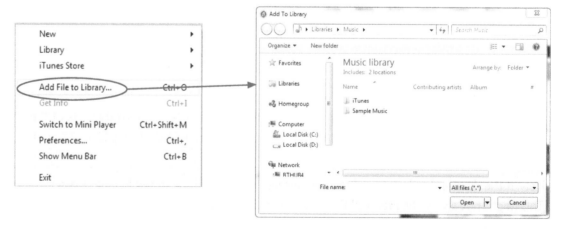

This is essentially the same feature in most programs that access files on a Windows PC. Developers do not write these types of functions themselves but use the Application Programming Interface (API) provided by Windows to use standard functionality. Why re-invent the wheel?

If you write a program that you want to run in a particular operating system then there will be plug-in modules of code already written for you, which you can use in your program. These pre-written modules of code are called library programs and are part of the system software along with the operating system. **Library programs** are modules of code that can be used in your programs. For example, if you write a program to work in Windows you can build in standard functionality such as the Open File dialogue box rather than writing it yourself.

Programming languages will also have library software that has been written for programmers to use in their programs. These are commonly used functionality. In Delphi programs, for example, statements like "Uses StrUtils" will import procedures that have already been written, in this case all the string handling functions. The programmer can use all the string handling functions without having to code them again.

The advantages of using library programs are:

- they perform standard functionality in a way users expect it to
- they have already been written for you so it saves time
- the routines have already been tested
- they can be called from anywhere in your program

Open source program code

Not all programs are copyrighted. There are many programs that programmers freely share; these are called **Open Source** programs. Open Source software is governed by the Open Source Initiative, which says:

- software is licensed for use but there is no charge for the licence. Anyone can use it
- Open Source software must be distributed with the source code so anyone can modify it
- developers can sell the software they have created
- any new software created from Open Source software must also be "open". This means that it must be distributed or sold in a form that other people can read and also edit

Using existing Open Source programs means you don't have to develop the algorithm and code yourself, just adapt it. However, although in theory it has already been tested, you cannot guarantee it works and there may not be much support for the program that you are adapting.

Other sources

As well as these specific categories of external sources there are many other sources of code that can be used. There are many web sites offering solutions to coding problems and also significant functionality that can be downloaded free of charge or for a price, which can be included in web sites or programs. One example is the shopping cart functionality for a web site that sells things. You can get Open Source code for this or buy a module you can add into your own system. Obviously you need to be aware of how the software is licensed if you are going to re-sell your own product!

Evaluating the Effectiveness of Programs

> **The AQA specification says that students should:**
>
> - be able to evaluate the effectiveness of computer programs/solutions

Programs or computer systems are evaluated in terms of their **effectiveness**, usability and maintainability.

Effectiveness could also be called usefulness or helpfulness. The effectiveness of a computer system could also be described as how successfully it meets the user's requirements. How is this measured?

As we saw in the *Chapter 4: Software Development Lifecycle*, one of the first steps in developing a computer program or system is to define exactly what the user needs it to do. The Requirements Specification is a key document that essentially lists success criteria. This is the list of things the program must do in order to be judged successful. The customer will check the final program against the Requirements Specification to make sure that the developer has finished the job.

Success criteria for a program should be specific, measurable requirements. For example, an electronic timetable package for a school might have the following requirements:

- Teachers can select a date
- Teachers can select a class
- Absence codes can be entered for each student listed

These are all specific things that the final program must do. You can tell if a requirement/success criteria is specific and measureable if you can say "yes, the program does this" or "no, it doesn't do that". If your criteria are a bit vague, so you end up looking at the program and saying "it sort of does this", or "I'm not really sure if it does that", then the criteria probably aren't specific enough.

Some examples of success criteria that are **not specific enough** are:

- It must be user-friendly
- It must be easy to use
- It must generate a report

If you catch yourself writing these for controlled assessments then try to think about what "user-friendly" and "easy to use" really means! For example, you could say that your program should have navigation buttons or use icons instead of text or use menus. Instead of a very general "generate a report" make sure you clearly state what the report is on, for example, "generate a report showing average attendance per student, ordered by surname".

Glossary of Terms

Variables, Data Types and Constants

Identifier	A unique name for something (variable, constant, program, procedure etc.) within the program.
Constant	A named value within a program that is assigned a specific value. Its value does not change while the program is running.
Variable	An identifier associated with a particular memory location, used to store data. Its value may change as the program is run and new values are assigned to it.
Data Type	A formal description of the type of data being stored in a variable. It defines the amount of memory required and the type of operations that can be performed on that variable.
Integer	Data type for whole numbers, typically uses 2 or 4 bytes.
Real/Float	Data type for fractional numbers, typically uses 4 or 8 bytes.
Character	Data type for a single character, typically uses 1 byte.
String	Data type for text, more than one character. Usually uses 1 byte per character.
Boolean	True or false. Typically uses 1 byte (even though one bit would do!)
Assignment	When a variable is given a value e.g. `Total ← Num1 + Num2`
Initialisation	Setting the starting values of variables explicitly.

Program Structure

Algorithm	A series of instructions that solves a problem in a finite number of steps and that always ends.
Pseudocode	A way of writing an algorithm that is close to actual programming language, using coding-style constructs such as IF...THEN...ELSE, loops and array notation as appropriate.
Boolean Expression	An expression that is true or false. For example: `continue="Y"` Expressions can be more complex, containing several parts: `((continue="Y") or (continue="y"))and (tries<10)`
Logical operators	NOT, AND, OR. Used in conditions/Boolean expressions.
Sequence	Where instructions are executed one after another in series.
Selection	Where the program will execute certain instructions based on conditions. Selection statements include: IF...THEN...ELSE and CASE...OF to select which commands to execute.

Iteration	Where a program will execute a group of instructions zero or more times based on a condition. FOR loops will execute instructions a specific number of times, REPEAT...UNTIL loops for one or more times and WHILE...DO loops for zero or more times.
Condition	A Boolean expression that controls an iteration or selection statement. For example, `REPEAT...UNTIL X=10` (X=10 is the condition).
Structure Chart	A diagram that shows how a module of code breaks down into smaller modules. Shows sequence, selection and iteration. For example: Jackson Structure Diagrams.
Flowchart	A diagram using commonly defined symbols to express an algorithm.

Procedures and Functions

Procedure	A block of code that performs a specific task. It has an identifier by which it can be called from within the program. Parameters can be passed into it. It may return one or more values.
Function	A block of code that always returns a single value. It has an identifier by which it can be called from within the program. Parameters can be passed into it. It can be used in an expression.
Parameter	A variable whose value is being passed into a function or procedure.
Parameter Passing	The process by which values of variables are passed into a function/procedure when the function/procedure is called.
Actual Parameter	The variable used in the main program when the function/procedure is called.
Formal Parameter	The variable used in the function/procedure code for the duration of this function/procedure running. It will take the value passed into it when the function/procedure is called.
Return Value	The result that is returned from a function or procedure. Can be any data type.
Built-In Procedure	The functions that the programming language already has coded for you to use. Standard functionality such as writing to the screen or reading from the keyboard.
Built-In Function	The standard functions that the programming language already has coded for you to use. For example, string handling functions and mathematical functions.
Scope of a Variable	The code blocks in which a variable is recognised and can be used. Will be local or global.
Global Variable	A variable that is declared in the main program and can be accessed anywhere in the program.
Local Variable	A variable that is declared within a function/procedure so it can only be accessed within that function or procedure.

Error Types and Error Handling

Syntax	A set of rules that defines how program statements must be written in order for the translator to understand them.
Syntax Errors	An error in the format of the program statements such as missing semicolons or keywords spelt incorrectly.
Logic Errors	An error in the algorithm that means the outcome is not as expected, even though the program will run.
Run-time Errors	An error that occurs after the program has started running because the program cannot perform the command for some reason. For example, division by zero or running out of memory.
Error Handling	Coding that protects the program from runtime errors by pre-empting possible errors triggered by issues outside of the scope of the program code. For example, inappropriate user input, opening missing files or a division that may result in a division by zero error.
Trace Tables	A manual way of tracking progress through an algorithm before it is coded. It tracks the changing values of variables through the code.
IDE	Integrated Development Environment. A programming environment that provides features such as: code editing, debugging help and run-time diagnostics.

External Data Sources

Text File	A file that can be read in a text editor and contains only ASCII characters such as numbers, letters and punctuation. Structured in lines.
Comma-Separated Value File	A text file that has multiple values on each line of text, separated by commas, so each line is in effect a record. It can be read in a text editor but also interpreted as separate fields by database and spreadsheet applications.
File of Records	A file of structured records where each field is named and has a data type. Cannot be viewed in a text editor.
Database	A file of records. Can be a relational database with multiple tables of related records or could just be a flat file/spreadsheet database.

External Code Sources

API	Application Programming Interface. The interface provided by operating systems for programmers to create their own applications that run on it. Includes library programs for programmers to use.
Library Programs	The systems software programs provided by the operating system so application programmers don't have to re-write basic functionality such as browsing for and opening a file. For example, dynamic link library files (.dll) in Windows.
Open Source Programs	Programs that are shared free of charge by developers and can be used in other programs as long as the resulting product is also Open Source.

Data Structures

Data Structures	Temporary structures in main memory that hold multiple data items while a program is running. For example, an array or record.
User-Defined Types	A data structure that is created by the programmer, which can then be used for variables. For example, a type called "TStudent" defines a record structure for any student; the variables "SixthFormStudent" and "GCSEStudent" can then be declared with this data type.
Array	A collection of data items with the same data type, which are grouped together under a single identifier. Individual data items are accessed using a subscript/index.
Subscript/Index	The numerical reference to a single data item within an array e.g. Numbers[1], where 1 is the subscript or index.

Sample Questions

These questions are similar to the ones you may see in the exam. Good answers to these, along with exam hints and tips, can be found at the end of the book.

1 The pseudocode below represents a function called `ArrayAverage`.

   `ArrayAverage` is used to find the average value stored in an array, where the average is the total of the numbers in the array divided by the number of numbers in the array.

   Note: line numbers have been shown but are not part of the function.

```
1    FUNCTION ArrayAverage(numbers)
2        total ← 0
3        FOR i ← 1 TO LEN(numbers)
4            total ← total + numbers[i]
5        ENDFOR
6        RETURN total/LEN(numbers)
7    ENDFUNCTION
```

(a) How many parameters does the function ArrayAverage have?   [1]

(b) This function uses iteration. Give the line number on which iteration starts.   [1]

(c) This function uses variable assignment.
     Give the line number in the function where variable assignment is first used.   [1]

(d) The variable i in this algorithm only has scope between lines 3 and 5.
     Explain with reference to the variable i what scope means.   [1]

2 (a) Write a program for a guessing game (using pseudocode or a flowchart) that does the following:

   • Assigns the word "cat" to a variable called answer
   • Assigns the user's input to a variable called guess
   • If the user correctly guesses "cat" then the program outputs "Correct", otherwise the program lets the user guess again
   • The game continues until the user guesses correctly   [6]

(b) The programmer wants to improve the game.
     State **two** simple changes that they could make to the game to improve it.   [2]

3 Give **two** reasons why programmers use procedures.   [2]

4 The pseudocode below shows a function that is used to work out if a person is entitled to a discount on bus season ticket pricing, based on their age:

```
1    FUNCTION discount(x)
2       IF x > 65 THEN
3           RETURN 1
4       ELSE
5           IF x < 16 THEN
6               RETURN -1
7           ELSE
8               RETURN 0
9           ENDIF
10      ENDIF
11   ENDFUNCTION
```

(a) The function discount returns an integer value.
Explain why a Boolean return value could not have been used. [1]

(b) Each of the following expressions evaluates to an integer. Give the integer value for each:

(i) discount(78) [1]

(ii) discount(13) [1]

(c) This function uses selection.
Give the line number on which selection starts. [1]

(d) The pseudocode above does not return the correct result for a 16 year old.
They should get discount if they are 16 or younger.

(i) What value does discount(16) currently return? [1]

(ii) What sort of error is this? [1]

(iii) Which line of code must be changed and what should it be changed to? [2]

5 A programmer is writing a software package to run on a specific operating system.
The programmer can use library programs provided by the operating system as external sources of code to perform standard functionality, such as saving a file.

Give two reasons why the programmer may want to use this external source of code. [2]

Appendix 1: Answers to Sample Questions

These answers are good responses to the questions that cover the mark scheme but probably give more detail than absolutely necessary – you want to make sure you get the marks so don't be too minimalist. Hints and tips on how to approach answers are in the grey boxes like this:

> ✱ *When you answer the questions you don't know what the mark scheme is going to say – you have to give all the information that is relevant in clear and concise phrases. Notice how many marks there are; if it is a 2 mark question try to make three specific points in response*

Answering Longer Exam Questions

With questions worth more than one mark it is important to make sure you answer the question fully. This is a method that may help you. It's called **BUMP**.

- **B**ox the keywords that say what you have to do, e.g. State..., Describe..., Explain...
- **U**nderline the bit you have to do it to, e.g. Describe advantages of using a computer system....
- **M**ake sure there isn't another bit to the question, e.g. and the need for this system to be reliable.
- **P**lan your answer, don't just start writing.

Some questions will state:

"In this question you will be marked on your ability to use good English, to organise information clearly and to use specialist vocabulary where appropriate."

You don't have to write an essay though – you can use **headings** and **bullet points** as long as these are written in good English.

Chapter 1: Fundamentals Of Computing

1

	Input	Output
Microphone	✓	
LED (light emitting diode)		✓
Barcode scanner	✓	
Speaker		✓
Actuator		✓

[5]

2 (i) The organisers can communicate with thousands of people at the same time by tweeting information to followers. The information can be spread much more quickly as members re-tweet to friends.

(ii) Social networking sites are accessed by many people using smart mobile phones. Even as things are changing at the protest, people can be updated on their phones.

(iii) Social networking sites would allow the organisers to post different media such as pictures, maps, videos and descriptions. They could share directions and maps easily as well as video clips to persuade people to take part.

[6]

> ✱ *For these questions, use structure to make it obvious that you have addressed everything in the question*

3 Fred is right because:

- The environment is affected by pollution from cars. If more people can work at home there will be less pollution.

- Computers managing car engines make them much more efficient – so reduce pollution.

- Computers are used to monitor and analyse the environment accurately over time, giving us a better picture of what is happening to the environment and what needs to be addressed

Priti is right because:

- Manufacturing computers generates pollution, which damages the environment.

- Computers contain some components that are damaging to the environment if they are not recycled properly.

- People are working individually at home because of better communications technology and computers, so people are heating and lighting many homes instead of one office, which would be greener   [6]

4 (i)   By installing software on their PC from a CD borrowed from a friend. They haven't bought a licence. This is an illegal copy of software protected by copyright.

   (ii) Downloading sounds/pictures/video from sites they know are breaking the copyright. Downloading is making an illegal copy.   [4]

Chapter 2: Hardware

1 (a)   ROM is Read Only Memory.

   (b)   RAM is volatile, ROM is non-volatile, i.e. retains its contents when power is switched off.

   (c)   It stores the start-up program needed when the computer is turned on, the "bootstrap loader". Stored on ROM because it is non-volatile.   [3]

2 (a)   RAM is used to hold programs that are currently running, and the data being used by the program.   [2]

   (b)   (i)   What it is: An area of the hard disk that acts like main memory.
               Why necessary: A computer has many programs running at any one time. These must all be in main memory. Virtual memory is needed if there is not enough main memory for all the programs that need to run.   [3]

         (ii) How used: If there is not enough main memory, parts of the programs can be stored in virtual memory, an area of the hard disc. Sections of the program are copied to main memory as required. Complete sections no longer need to be in main memory.   [3]

   (c)   Main memory has a faster access speed than virtual memory. More main memory means that more programs will fit in main memory, so virtual memory will be accessed less frequently and programs will run faster.   [2]

   (d)   Upgrade the processor chip to one with a higher clock speed. This will mean the computer can execute instructions quicker and improve its performance.   [2]

> ✱ *State the component to upgrade and then how it will increase performance.*
> *"This means that..." is a useful phrase – state something and then explain why*

3 Non-volatile storage used for long term storage of files. E.g. hard disk [2]

4 (a) A hard disk on their home computer to store files such as the operating system, applications and the presentation for school while they are working on it.

A USB memory stick to take a copy of the presentation to school. [4]

(b)

	Capacity
CD	700 MB
DVD ROM	16 GB
Hard disk	4 TB
USB memory stick	256 GB

[4]

5 Processors are becoming more powerful – they can execute more instructions per second on the same sized chip for the same price. The cost of main memory and secondary memory is reducing in price and increasing in capacity.

This means that portable gadgets could be made much cheaper so computers can be embedded into things like fridge doors and table tops or even into clothes and sunglasses.

Another effect is to increase the power and functionality on gadgets, rather than making them cheaper and smaller. For example, mobile phones and cameras are effectively mini-computers now. We can browse the internet and run apps on our phones. Cameras can interact directly with computers or social networking sites and cloud storage. [6]

> ✳ *In questions like this make sure you use the correct technical terms and make your answer precise. Give specific examples as part of the explanation. Don't waffle!*

Chapter 3: Data Representation

1 (a) 182 (128+32+16+4+2) [1]

(b) 137/16 = 8.56 so 8 groups of 16, 8 x 16 = 128, 137 - 128 = 9, Hex = 89 [2]

(c) 2 x 16 = 32, C represents 12 so denary is 32 + 12 = 44 [2]

(d) People find long numbers hard to remember, especially in binary. Hex represents the same number but is much easier for people to use. Because 1 Hex digit represents 4 bits it is an easy conversion to binary. [1]

2 1024 x 1024 (2^{20}, 1,048,576 or 1024x1024 are all correct answers.) [1]

3 The ASCII code for "A" is 1000001

(a) 128 (7 bits, so 0 to 127 gives 128 different numbers) [1]

(b) 1000100 (if A is 1 then D is 4, the codes are in sequence) [1]

4 The sound wave hits the microphone which detects it.
The wave is converted into an electrical signal.
The signal is sampled at regular intervals to get values, which are rounded to a level.
These rounded samples are stored as binary in a sound file.   [3]

5 This will increase the file size because increasing the resolution increases the number of pixels
that must be stored.   [2]

Chapter 4: Software Development Lifecycle

1 Alpha testing is done in-house. It is when programmers test each other's programs and give
feedback on any problem found.

Beta testing is done on an almost complete piece of software. It is when it is given to a sample group
of customers to try out in the real-world. It means the software gets tested on lots of different sorts
of hardware and with lots of real data.

Key differences are:

* Alpha testing is done in-house by programmers in a test lab.
* Beta testing is done by potential users in the real world.
* Alpha testing will use a limited selection of hardware and data.
* Beta testing will expose the software to real-world data, users inputting unexpected data
  and many more hardware platforms.
* Alpha testing can be done at various points in the development on specific parts of the system.
  Beta testing will be the complete package almost ready for release.   [6]

2 (i)   Corrective maintenance: They might find bugs that need fixing.
         For example, it won't print the receipt properly.

   (ii) Adaptive maintenance: The requirements for the business may change over time, which means
         the software requirements may change.
         For example, the company starts offering an online booking system for its cars.

   (iii) Perfective maintenance: The performance may need improving.
         For example, as the company grows the system slows down so it needs improving.   [6]

3 Any three of the following:
   * Interview key people/stakeholders.
   * Interview the people who manage the point of sale and stock control to find out what they need
     the system to do.
   * Use a questionnaire to get more data about the point of sale requirements. Ask all the checkout
     staff what they like and dislike about the current system, and what they would like it to do.
   * Observe staff using the current system. Watch someone doing stock control and someone working
     on the point of sale to see what problems they have and how they actually work.
   * Collect existing documentation to show what reports are currently used, layouts and data formats.
     For example, get sample checkout receipts and stock reports.   [6]

4

Test purpose	Test data	Expected outcome
Quantity text box accepts valid data	37	Data accepted
Quantity text box does not accept numbers > 50	51	Error message
Quantity text box does not accept invalid characters	zero	Error message

[7]

> ✱ Test data should cover the following:
>
> **Valid** data that should be accepted – any number between 1 and 50 in this case
>
> **Extremes** are good data inputs to test – 1 and 50 are valid but at the extremes of the range here
>
> **Invalid** data that is outside the allowed range – any number less than 1 or greater than 50 in this case

5 The programmer could use the Waterfall Model to work through a series of well-defined stages in sequence to generate the software. This has the benefit of being well established and very well structured so if she is working on a large project with many other programmers, this would be a good model to follow. The disadvantage of this model is its inflexibility. If issues are found in a later stage, it is difficult and expensive to go back to an earlier stage. Another issue with this model is the lack of client involvement after the Analysis stage so issues may not be picked up until evaluation.

An alternative is the Agile Model, which has similar stages but does not perform each one to completion in one go. The process is iterative and builds the level of detail in a series of prototypes until the product is complete. The main advantage is that the client is involved at each stage and gives feedback on each prototype so the end product is likely to be what they want. The iterative approach also makes it easier to address issues as they occur. The disadvantage of this model is that the client involvement can change the requirements as the project progresses. [8]

Chapter 5: Networking

1 (a) Any two of the following:

The performance for individual computers is more consistent because each computer has its own cable connecting it to the central device, not a shared cable like a bus or ring.

Cable problems don't affect as many people as in a bus or ring because if one cable fails it will only affect the one computer it is connecting to the central device.

It is easy to add new devices to the network because you just have to plug another cable into the central device.

It is more secure than a bus or ring because the connection between the computer and the central device is not shared by other computers. [4]

(b) A protocol is a set of rules that defines how devices communicate.
For example, IP (Internet Protocol) [2]

(c) The end that wants to communicate sends a signal to the other device.

The other device sends this signal back to the first one with an acknowledgement.

The first one then acknowledges this.

The devices can now communicate. [3]

(d) For each of the following events statements associated with a client-server network, indicate whether it is true or false by ticking **one** column in each row. [4]

	Event	True	False
(i)	Querying a database is a server-side program	✓	
(ii)	Validation only happens on the client-side		✓
(iii)	The browser runs on a client	✓	
(iv)	Java applets are embedded in the server-side code		✓

2 Sam will have to code the system in two parts. The client end will be the user application that runs in the browser when the customer places an order. The server end will be at the bakery. In a stand alone system the whole program would be in one place.

The client server system must manage the network connection whereas the standalone system does not have a network involved.

A client-server system must manage multiple users at the same time as many customers might be online using it. A standalone system has just one user at any time.

As the customer may be sending card details over the network, Sam will need to make sure this is secure. In a standalone system the data is not being sent over the internet. [6]

✱ *In these questions your spelling, grammar and use of appropriate technical terms will matter.*

3 (a) Sharing folders and files so you can access files anywhere on the network from any computer and different people can access these files as needed

Software can be sent out to all the computers from a central server rather than having to install it on each individual computer

The company can have one connection to the internet, which can be shared by all the computers on the network. [3]

(b) A client is a computer used for end-user tasks, in this case they will run the applications used to hire out equipment. It will make requests to the server for data and services. [2]

(c) Servers are computers with a specialised role, to provide data and services to client computers on the network.

There may be different servers for different roles:
- email server to deliver email services
- print server to store and manage documents being sent to printers on the network
- web server to host the hire company's website for external customers
- file server to store the company's data and other files [4]

Chapter 6: Databases

1 (a) OwnerID
   It uniquely identifies each owner, more than one owner may have the same name [2]

   (b) Spot   Jessica   Mason

   Jasper   Dev   Patel

   Desmond   Jessica   Mason [3]

   (c) Insert into PET(PetID, Name, Animal, OwnerID)
   values(49, "Ginger", "Cat", 6); [3]

   > * As all of the fields are being assigned a value this is also a valid answer:
   >
   > Insert into PET
   > values(49, "Ginger", "Cat", 6);

49	Ginger	Cat	6

   (d) OwnerId is the foreign key in the Pet table. It is also the primary key in the Owner table so it is being used to create a relationship between the two tables. This is used to get data about the owner of each pet. [3]

   > * Use your standard definition for a foreign key here but apply it to the scenario given. Make reference to the specific fields for this database.

2 A flat file is like one big table storing all the data about customers and what they have bought. This means that the customer details will be repeated every time that they buy something. This duplicated data is redundant and can lead to data inconsistency when records are updated.

   A relational database stores the data in multiple tables. Each logical entity in the system (customer and purchase in this case) becomes a separate table so data about customers is only stored once and details of each purchase is only stored once. The tables are connected together with a relationship between the primary key of the customer table (e.g. CustID) and the foreign key in the purchases table (also CustID).

   The relational database is a better solution because it minimises data redundancy, which in turn means there will not be data inconsistency when data is updated.

   The relational database only stores data once so it will also take less space than the flat file solution. [6]

3

Database Term	Description
(a) Record	Can store all the data about a specific person
(b) Foreign Key	Must be a primary key in another table
(c) Primary Key	Uniquely identifies a record
(d) Index	Used to speed up searches for specific records

(4)

Chapter 7: Programming Concepts

1 (a)   1   *(numbers)* [1]

(b)   3   *(where the FOR loop starts)* [1]

(c)   2   *(total ← 0)* [1]

(d)   Scope is the area of code in which a variable has significance, where it can be referenced.

In this case i is only used within the FOR loop as a counter, it cannot be referenced outside this loop. [1]

2 (a)   There are several ways of doing this. Here are two solutions: [6]

```
answer ← "cat"                    answer ← "cat"
REPEAT                            guess ← userinput
   guess ← userinput             WHILE answer ≠ guess THEN
   IF guess = answer THEN            Output "Try again"
      Output "Correct"              guess ← userinput
   ELSE                          ENDWHILE
      Output "Try again"         Output "Correct"
   ENDIF
UNTIL guess = answer
```

(b)   Limit the number of guesses
Add scoring – score more points if you guess in fewer tries [2]

3   The same code can be re-used in different parts of the program without having to rewrite it.
The code is easier to understand so it is easier to debug and maintain. [2]

4 (a)   The function will return one of three values (0, -1, 1)
A boolean must be true or false so cannot be used [1]

(b)   (i)   1   *(because x > 65 is true)* [1]

(ii)   -1   *(because x > 65 is false and x < 16 is true)* [1]

(c)   2   *(the start of the IF statement)* [1]

(d)   The pseudocode above does not return the correct result for a 16-year old. They should get discount if they are 16 or younger.

(i)   0 [1]

(ii)   Logic error [1]

(iii)   Change line 5 to: IF x ≤ 16 THEN [2]

> ✱ *Although AQA use standard pseudocode in their exam papers, you can use any form of pseudocode as long as it makes sense. You can write <= instead of ≤ for example.*

5   It will save time as the code has already been written.
It has already been tested. [2]

3.1.1 CONSTANTS, VARIABLES AND DATA TYPES	
understand what is meant by the terms data and information	Ch3 p41
be able to describe the difference between a constant and a variable	Ch7 p95-99
understand when to use constants and variables in problem solving scenarios	
understand the different data types available to them. As a minimum, students should know about integer, Boolean, real, character and string data types and how these are represented in the programming language(s) they are using	
be able to explain the purpose of data types within code	
understand and be able to program with 1 and 2 dimensional arrays	Ch7 p99-101
be able to use NOT, AND and OR when creating Boolean expressions and have experience in using these operators within coded solutions	Ch7 p102

3.1.2 STRUCTURES	
be able to explain what a data structure is	Ch7 p126-127
be able to produce their own data types that go beyond the built in structures of the language(s) they are using, such as arrays or lists. These could include, for example, records in Delphi, structs in C or classes in Python and Java. The actual structures would depend on the language(s) being used by the students	
understand and be able to explain why data structures can make coding a solution simpler	

3.1.3 PROGRAM FLOW CONTROL	
understand the need for structure when designing coded solutions to problems	Ch7 p107-112
understand how problems can be broken down into smaller problems and how these steps can be represented by the use of devices such as flowcharts and structure diagrams	
understand and be able to describe the basic building blocks of coded solutions (i.e. sequencing, selection and iteration)	Ch7 p103-105
know when to use the different flow control blocks (i.e. sequencing, selection and iteration) to solve a problem	

3.1.4 PROCEDURES AND FUNCTIONS	
understand what procedures and functions are in programming terms	Ch7 p113-115
know when the use of a procedure or function would make sense and would simplify the coded solution	
know how to write and use their own simple procedures and functions	
know about and be able to describe common built in functions in their chosen language(s)	Ch7 p116-117
use common built-in functions in their chosen language(s) when coding solutions to problems	
understand what a parameter is when working with procedures and functions	Ch7 p115
know how to use parameters when creating efficient solutions to problems	
understand the concepts of parameters and return values when working with procedures and functions	

3.1.5 SCOPE OF VARIABLES, CONSTANTS, FUNCTIONS AND PROCEDURES	
know what is meant by the scope of a variable, constant, function or procedure	Ch7 p116-117
be able to identify what value a particular variable will hold at a given point in the code	

3.1.6 ERROR HANDLING	
be able to discuss and identify the different types of errors that can occur within code (i.e. syntax, run-time and logical)	Ch7 p118-119
understand that some errors will occur during the execution of the code	
understand that some errors can be detected and corrected during the coding stage	Ch7 p123-125
know how to detect errors at execution time and how to handle those errors to prevent the program from crashing where desirable	
understand that computer programs can be developed with tools to help the programmer detect and deal with errors (e.g. Watch, Breakpoint, Step)	
be able to use trace tables to check their code for errors	Ch7 p120

3.1.7 HANDLING EXTERNAL DATA	
know how to use an external text file to read and write data in a way that is appropriate for the programming language(s) used and the problem being solved	Ch7 p127-129
know how to read and write data from an external database in a way that is appropriate for the programming anguage(s) used and the problem being solved	Ch7 p130
3.1.8 COMPUTER STRUCTURE	
3.1.8.1 Systems	
be able to define a computer system (i.e. hardware and software working together to create a working solution)	Ch1 p1
understand and be able to discuss the importance of computer systems to the modern world	
understand that computer systems must be reliable and robust and be able to discuss the reasons why this is important	Ch1 p2-3
3.1.8.2 Hardware	
be able to describe and explain the fundamental pieces of hardware required to make a functioning computer system	Ch1 p1
be able to discuss how developments in different hardware technologies (including memory and processor) are leading to exciting innovative products being created, e.g. in the mobile and gaming industries	Ch2 p21-22
be able to categorise devices as input or output depending on their function	Ch2 p22-26
3.1.8.3 CPU	
be able to describe the purpose of the processor (CPU)	Ch2 p9-10
understand how different components link to a processor (ROM, RAM, I/O, storage, etc)	Ch2 p12
be able to explain the effect of common CPU characteristics on the performance of the processor. These should include clock speed, number of cores and cache size/types	Ch2 p10-12
3.1.8.4 Memory	
know the differences between non-volatile and volatile memory	Ch2 p15
understand the purpose of both types of memory and when each should be used	Ch2 p13-14
be able to explain the concept that data and instructions are stored in memory and processed by the CPU	
be able to explain the purpose of virtual memory and cache memory	Ch2 p14, 11
3.1.8.4 Secondary Storage	
understand what secondary storage is and be able to explain why it is required	Ch2 p15-21
be able to describe the most common types of secondary storage	
understand how optical media, magnetic media and solid state work	
3.1.9 ALGORITHMS	
understand that algorithms are computational solutions that always finish and return an answer	Ch7 p106
be able to interpret simple algorithms to deduce their function	
be able to create algorithms to solve simple problems	
be able to detect and correct errors in simple algorithms	Ch7 p120-121
3.1.10 DATA REPRESENTATION	
understand that computers use the binary alphabet to represent all data and instructions	Ch3 p31
understand the terms bit, nibble, byte, kilobyte, megabyte, gigabyte and terabyte	
understand that a binary code could represent different types of data such as text, image, sound, integer, date, real number	Ch3 p35-40
understand how binary can be used to represent positive whole numbers (up to 255)	Ch3 p32
understand how sound and bitmap images can be represented in binary	Ch3 p39-40
understand how characters are represented in binary and be familiar with ASCII and its limitations	Ch3 p37-38
understand why hexadecimal number srepresentation is often used and know how to convert between binary, denary and hexadecimal	Ch3 p34-35

3.1.11 SOFTWARE DEVELOPMENT LIFECYCLE	
understand the software development life cycle	Ch4 p45-48
be able to explain what commonly occurs at each stage of the software development life cycle	
be able to identify at which stage of the software development life cycle a given step would occur	
understand that there are several lifecycle models that can be used (eg cyclical, waterfall, spiral)	Ch4 p48-50
be able to discuss the advantages and disadvantages of these lifecycle models	
3.1.11.1 Prototyping	
understand what prototyping is	Ch4 p51
be able to discuss the advantages and disadvantages of using prototyping when developing solutions	
have experience of using prototyping to create solutions to simple problems	
3.1.12 Application Testing	
understand the need for rigorous testing of coded solutions	Ch4 p52
understand the different types of tests that can be used, including unit/modular testing	Ch4 p52-53
be able to create suitable test plans and carry out suitable testing to demonstrate their solutions work as intended	Ch4 p53-54
be able to hand test simple code designs/algorithms using trace tables	Ch7 p120-121 Ch4 p52
3.1.13 NETWORKING	
understand what a computer network is	Ch5 p59-62
be able to discuss the advantages and disadvantages of using a computer network	
be able to describe and explain the bus, ring and star networking topologies	
be able to discuss the advantages and disadvantages of each of these topologies	
3.1.13.1 Client Server	
understand the client-server model	Ch5 p63
be able to explain, in simple terms, the handshake process used in most modern networking protocols	Ch5 p66
be able to explain how coding for a client-server model is different from coding for a stand-alone application	Ch5 p64-65
3.1.13.2 Web Application Concepts	
understand the concept of coding at the server and client end	Ch5 p66-69
know what can be coded at the server end	
know what can be coded at the client end	
have experience of coding solutions to simple web application problems	Ch5 p69-75
3.1.14 USE OF EXTERNAL CODE SOURCES	
know of the existence of external code sources	Ch7 p132-133
know how to integrate code from these sources into their own code	
be able to explain the advantages and disadvantages of using such sources	
3.1.15 DATABASE CONCEPTS	
understand the basic concepts of a relational database as a data store	Ch6 p79
be able to explain the terms record, field, table, query, primary key, relationship, index and search criteria	Ch6 p81-82
3.1.15.1 Query Methods (SQL)	
be able to create simple SQL statements to extract, add and edit data stored in databases	Ch6 p84-87
have experience of using these SQL statements from within their own coded systems	Ch6 p88
3.1.15.2 Connecting to Databases from Applications and Web Based Apps	
be able to use databases from within their own web based applications	Ch6 p89-91
3.1.16 THE USE OF COMPUTER TECHNOLOGY IN SOCIETY	
be able to evaluate the effectiveness of computer programs/solutions	Ch7 p132
be able to evaluate the impact of and issues related to the use of computer technology in society	Ch1 p3-5

Index

Lightning Source UK Ltd.
Milton Keynes UK
UKOW07f2120050515

250907UK00009B/73/P